Donated to
Maddux Library
Trinity University

THE MARRS McLEAN TRUST,
established for the benefit
of Trinity University by
MRS. VERNA HOOKS McLEAN

SELECTED PAPERS FROM THE SECOND WORLD CONGRESS FOR SOVIET AND EAST EUROPEAN STUDIES
GARMISCH-PARTENKIRCHEN
SEPTEMBER 30-OCTOBER 4, 1980

Sponsored by

INTERNATIONAL COMMITTEE FOR SOVIET AND EAST EUROPEAN STUDIES
and
DEUTSCHE GESELLSCHAFT FÜR OSTEUROPAKUNDE

General Editor
Roger E. Kanet
University of Illinois at Urbana-Champaign

EDITORIAL COMMITTEE MEMBERS

Patrick L. Alston, Bowling Green State University
Oskar Anweiler, Ruhr-Universität Bochum
Evelyn C. Bristol, University of Illinois at Urbana-Champaign
Georg Brunner, Universität Würzburg
Marianna Tax Choldin, University of Illinois at Urbana-Champaign
R.W. Davies, The University of Birmingham
Dennis J. Dunn, Southwest Texas State University
R.C. Elwood, Carleton University
Zbigniew M. Fallenbuchl, University of Windsor
Frank Y. Gladney, University of Illinois at Urbana-Champaign
Bohdan Harasymiw, The University of Calgary
Roger E. Kanet, University of Illinois at Urbana-Champaign
Thomas F. Magner, The Pennsylvania State University
Sidney Monas, The University of Texas at Austin
Temira Pachmuss, University of Illinois at Urbana-Champaign
Peter J. Potichnyj, McMaster University
T. Harry Rigby, Australian National University
Hans Rogger, University of California, Los Angeles
Gertrude Schroeder Greenslade, University of Virginia
Jane Shapiro Zacek, Governor's Office of Employee Relations (New York)
Günther Stökl, Universität Köln

EAST EUROPEAN LITERATURE

SELECTED PAPERS FROM THE SECOND WORLD CONGRESS
FOR SOVIET AND EAST EUROPEAN STUDIES

Edited by
Evelyn Bristol
University of Illinois at Urbana-Champaign

BERKELEY SLAVIC SPECIALTIES
Berkeley, 1982

Copyright © 1982 Berkeley Slavic Specialties
All Rights Reserved

"Introduction" © 1982 Evelyn Bristol; "Continuity and Discontinuity in the Poetry of Pavlo Tychyna" © 1982 George G. Grabowicz; "All of Alija's Women: Andrić's Realization of 'Ex Ponto' Visions" © 1982 Želimir Juričić; "The Contemporary Polish Historical Novel and Its Political Inspirations" © 1982 Jerzy R. Krzyzanowski; "The Mysterious and Irrational Elements in the Works of Mykhailo Kotsiubyns'kyi and Theodor Storm" © 1982 Myron E. Nowosad; "The Contemporary Czech Historical Novel and Its Political Inspiration" © 1982 Walter Schamschula; "History as Fiction: The Novels of Teodor Parnicki" © 1982 Wojciech Skalmowski; "The Party Guidance of a Soviet Literature: The Case of the Ukraine, 1968–1975" © 1982 Victor Swoboda.

PRINTED IN U.S.A.

ISBN 0-933884-26-5

CONTENTS

Foreword *by the General Editor* 7
Introduction *by Evelyn Bristol* 9
Continuity and Discontinuity in the Poetry of Pavlo Tychyna
   by George G. Grabowicz 13
All of Alija's Women: Andrić's Realization of "Ex Ponto" Visions
   by Želimir Juričić 23
The Contemporary Polish Historical Novel and Its Political Inspirations *by Jerzy R. Krzyżanowski* 33
The Mysterious and Irrational Elements in the Works of Mykhailo Kotsiubyns'kyi and Theodor Storm *by Myron E. Nowosad* 43
The Contemporary Czech Historical Novel and Its Political Inspiration *by Walter Schamschula* 57
History as Fiction: The Novels of Teodor Parnicki
   by Wojciech Skalmowski 69
The Party Guidance of a Soviet Literature: The Case of the Ukraine, 1968–1975 *by Victor Swoboda* 85

FOREWORD BY THE GENERAL EDITOR

The articles published in this volume have been selected from among those presented at the Second World Congress for Soviet and East European Studies, held in Garmisch-Partenkirchen, Federal Republic of Germany, September 30 – October 4, 1980. The Congress was sponsored by the International Committee for Soviet and East European Studies in conjunction with the Deutsche Gesellschaft für Osteuropakunde and was attended by well over 1,400 scholars from around the world.

Among the approximately five hundred formal papers and additional papers presented at the Congress, more than 150 were submitted for consideration to the editorial committee for the official English-language Congress publications. From among these a substantial number have been accepted for publication in the series of thirteen volumes to be published by Berkeley Slavic Specialties, (Berkeley, California, U.S.A.), Pergamon Press (New York, N.Y., U.S.A.), Russica Publishers (New York, N.Y., U.S.A.), Allen and Unwin (London, England), Praeger Publishers (New York, N.Y., U.S.A.), and Martinus Nijhoff Publishers (The Hague, The Netherlands). In addition, several other volumes are scheduled for publication in Germany.

As general editor of the series of English-language Garmisch Congress publications, I wish to express my sincere appreciation to all of the individuals and organizations that made the conference and the resulting publications possible. This includes the numerous organizations that provided financial support for the

Congress itself, the Executive Committee of the International Committee for Soviet and East European Studies (including the past president, Adam Bromke) and in particular, the members of the German Planning Committee who organized the Congress (including the chairman and current president of the International Committee, Oskar Anweiler). Finally, I wish to thank the Congress participants who submitted their papers for consideration, the members of the editorial committee that selected the essays to be included in the various volumes, and the editors of those volumes. Their contributions and cooperation have made possible the publication of this volume and the other volumes in the series.

Roger E. Kanet

*University of Illinois
 at Urbana-Champaign*

INTRODUCTION

East European literatures are still committed, as these articles by Western Slavic scholars show, to the enhancement of their national identities, but Eastern authors also participate in the complex trends of Western literature. The papers written for the conference at Garmisch-Partenkirchen were restricted in subject to the twentieth century, yet Eastern literatures are described here as having remained relatively Romantic in spirit. The traditional historical novel, which contributed so much to the establishment of cultural identities in the nineteenth century, is the subject of two articles. Avantgardistic, or neo-Romantic trends, which are also current in the East, are touched upon, but less often. In their quest for cultural self-awareness, East European authors depict or hint at both Eastern and Western military occupations; they pose problems in terms of moral, or even aesthetic, issues. But, no matter how variously those problems were conceived, they apparently tend now to be seen as a part of the nearly inescapable East-West opposition. A case in point is that of the Ukrainian poet Pavlo Tychyna, whose loyalty is claimed by both iron curtain and émigré critics; both sides discern a conflict in his work between "lyric" and "public" poetry, but neither will perceive his oeuvre as whole. In this divisive kind of atmosphere East European authors feel constrained to write about national and moral issues, and with an eye not only to posterity, but to tomorrow.

In Poland and in Czechoslovakia the traditional historical novel is described as having remained a viable, if not a popular, vehicle for national assertiveness. The glorification of the nation's past is still its main aim; local cultures are depicted as venerable compared with those of surrounding, or oppressor, nations. Józef Kraszewski, a Romantic, and Henryk Sienkiewicz, a nineteenth century positivist, still serve as models for more recent Polish historical novels. Their common subject is "the moral responsibility for the national destiny," as Jerzy Krzyżanowski writes in his article. Specific topics which they often treat are the relationship between church and state and the nature of political power itself. The Czech historical novel is somewhat more popular as a genre, but its uses of the past are shown to be analogous. Czech eulogies of the past perhaps place less stress on heroism; kings and queens are honored who were public servants. And Czech messianism is soberly associated with the distant Hussite period, rather than with the Romantic era. Even Socialist Realism has been used for the expression of Czech patriotism, and Czechs have sometimes encoded current messages in their historical novels. The East European historical novel is, nevertheless, everywhere understood to embody a universal need for freedom.

Other East European authors are described as appealing to broader Romantic premises. They rise above tyranny to strike at its putative handmaiden, rationalism. Their subjects are the nature of things and intimate human nature, psychology. Mykhailo Kotsiubyns'kyi is shown to have emerged from Realism; his impressionism serves a renewed sensitivity to the irrational, the wellspring of any Romantic tendency. He again cast an aura of supernatural significance on nature and hinted at metaphysical objections to injustice and death in what Realists had seen only as an ordered world. He is compared here with the German short story writer Theodor Storm, to whom some elements of Romantic philosophy still clung. Both authors paid superficial tribute to Realism but strove to win some psychic freedom from it through their reflections on the uncanny.

A Modernistic assertion of identity, at once personal and national, is seen in the historical novels of Teodor Parnicki, who has increasingly filtered history through his own conscious. Reared in Russia, but with a semi-Polish background, he chose to identify his destiny with Poland's. He turned to the historical novel, as did others, to exemplify the greatness of past eras, but his locales are often not specifically Polish. His idiosyncracy is that he portrays half-breeds who have struggled to achieve their own identity as being also the movers of history and thus the source of the glories of the human race. His many novels depict a world of interconnected spheres where far-flung characters are related to each other by family ties; together they are invincible and steer historical events. His later works are described, however, as tantamount to dialogues among factions within his own consciousness, perhaps seeking to weld themselves into an identity. A grandiose historical sweep unfolds in his oeuvre, but history becomes indistinguishable from his perception of it.

The subtleties of philosophical and literary trends can be foregone, as a study of the political control of Ukrainian literature shows, when the assertion of national identity is to be clear and practical. Allusions to a specific cultural heritage, such as the Zaporozhian Sech, are useful, but works which contain them are liable to unforeseen critical attacks. Religious reflections, speculations on nature, death, or any other ultimate realities, are similarly risky.

Yugoslav authors are now free from external pressure, but they remember foreign domination and are also frequently concerned with cultural identities. Ivo Andrić's oeuvre consists in the patient recreation of the past of Bosnia, manifestly with the humane purpose of reconciling its different ethnic groups, which have various Eastern and Western legacies. Andrić's early works are described here as a probing within the Bosnian identity of what appears to be a Romantic tendency: the idealization (or denigration) of women. Perhaps the impulse is rather the heritage of a semi-Eastern past? In any case, the depiction of Woman as mystery is overshadowed by a more universal theme: death and transience as the destiny of all. His fiction contrasts a teeming ethnicity on the surface to an undercurrent of emptiness and quandary. Thus history and philosophy (or religion) are shown throughout this volume to form a repertory of themes which are common to Eastern European literatures and which serve both for practical manoeuvres and in the creation of enduring works.

Evelyn Bristol

*University of Illinois
at Urbana-Champaign*

CONTINUITY AND DISCONTINUITY IN THE POETRY OF PAVLO TYCHYNA

GEORGE G. GRABOWICZ

The case of Pavlo Tychyna is both paradoxical and eminently revealing of the deep problems facing twentieth century Ukrainian literary history. There is, on the one hand, a general consensus (more pronounced in Soviet criticism and scholarship, but essentially shared by Western and émigré criticism) that Tychyna is the greatest Ukrainian poet of this century. At the same time there is little if any consensus on what constitutes the core of his poetic achievement. The problem is "resolved" precisely in the manner in which the great bulk of post-Revolutionary Ukrainian literature is approached: by a categorical and exclusionary ideological demarcation. Just as we now seem to have two Ukrainian literatures — to judge by contrasting Soviet with non-Soviet studies, histories, anthologies — so we seem to have two Tychynas, most commonly designated the "early" and the "late." What is so revealing and disturbing, to my mind, is not the very imposition of ideological criteria and thus the mechanical halving of the poet's work, but the inability of serious scholarship to come to grips with the problem and resolve the impasse. It would appear that neither side is capable of shedding its sectarian and, at the very least, normative thinking. The solitary exceptions tend to prove the rule.

The critical tradition of perceiving a break, a discontinuity, in Tychyna's poetry may well begin with M. Zerov who in an early article on his fellow "neo-classicist" M. Ryl's'kyi, commented in passing that Tychyna played all his trumps in his first collection, *Soniashni kliarnety,* and was subsequently forced to play a "weak and trumpless game."[1] What began as an aesthetic judgment (and here Zerov was clearly out of sympathy with Tychyna's poetics) soon became an overtly ideological one. As if in answer to official Soviet proclamations of Tychyna's newly found orthodoxy (especially after his *Partiia vede;* 1933), Ukrainian critics in the West announced his poetic demise. Thus E. Malaniuk set the tone by calling Tychyna's preceding collection, *Chernihiv* (1931), "a psychopathic collection of autoparodies."[2] Later, I. Koshelivets' spoke of Tychyna's transition to "Sovietism" as equivalent to his assuming the role ("mask") of a "loyal odist" and as signalling "the transformation of a genial poet into an irreproachable hack."[3] In his typical bardic and quasi-religious manner V. Barka cites (as do so many others) the last line of *Zamist' sonetiv i oktav* — "Khiba i sobi potsiluvat' pantofliu Papy?" — as proof of Tychyna's anguished prophecy of his imminent surrender and restructuring. According to this view "the red slipper which he kissed concealed in its fabric a poison which entered him like a spiritual paralysis and killed the orphean strings of his heart."[4] In short, balanced and reasoned analysis was replaced by the eminently presecular notion that the gift of poetry — like God's grace — was denied Tychyna after he abandoned the camp of the righteous. For its part, Soviet criticism was and remains remarkably parallel: it offers the teleological axiom that after various nationalist, "formalist" and "abstract humanist" waverings, Tychyna, with the guidance of the Party, of course, found the true path of socialist realism, Marxism-Leninism, socialist internationalism, and so forth. (At the end, Tychyna himself was one of those who maintained this.) While ideologically opposite, both perspectives share many of the same premises and structures of thought, most notably the perception of surface or manifest "ideology" as absolute, the reduction of the poetic statement to its political message, a normative and conservative aesthetics (significantly both Soviet and émigré critics found *Chernihiv*'s experimentation unacceptable), and the belief that Tychyna's poetic oeuvre is largely or even radically discontinuous.

A re-evaluation of our approach to Tychyna seems to me long overdue — especially since the canon of his poetry has recently been substantially filled in, most notably by two important publications, the unpublished and "forgotten" poetry in *V sertsi u moïm* and the long (though unfinished) "symphony" *Skovoroda*.[5] The issue is many-faceted, of course, but it seems that the question of continuity or discontinuity is central precisely because it subsumes both the historical dimension, that is, Tychyna's poetic evolution, and the analytic, that is the various levels of his poetry — formal, thematic, psychological, and so on. Through this focus, we can posit new criteria for understanding both the complex nature of his poetry and its periods. At the outset, of course, we must remove or bracket the ideological-political criterion since it is prescriptive and normative and not analytical; poetry, clearly, is not to be judged as if it were a political manifesto or slogan. (Such constituent aspects as censorship and self-censorship, sincerity and insincerity, should be considered, but within the proper framework.) Secondly, it must be recognized that the aesthetic judgment — which at its crudest is, for example, the opinion of many that Tychyna simply went bad, or as the epigram had it, "A Tychyna pyshe virshi, Ta vse hirshi, Ta vse hirshi" — is a synthetic judgment, one that derives from the polyphony of various relevant artistic, semantic and other criteria; while one can certainly evaluate different phases or periods, and say, for example, that *Pluh* (1920) is still good, but *Viter z Ukraïny* (1924) is already bad, an aesthetic judgment is not in and of itself sufficient basis for establishing continuity or discontinuity. When it *is* presented as such, the argument is based on taste, not on analysis.

The question of continuity or discontinuity in Tychyna can best be examined, I submit, by distinguishing and then analyzing three levels of his poetry: the manifest or thematic, the formal, and the level of symbols and of deeper structures. It goes without saying, of course, that these are often interconnected and hardly distinguishable, but they do offer a preliminary basis or schema for decoding his poetry's intricate system..

A first level therefore, the one on which a preponderant amount of attention has been focused, is that of surface significations, of pure signs; at its most obvious this is the overt political slogan, the rhetorical elaborations on the theme of "Partiia vede!" and the various paeans to Lenin, Stalin and the Soviet system. It is precisely here that discontinuity is so frequently perceived, for, so the argument is made, the early Tychyna, author of such poems as "Viina," "Zolotyi homin," "Pam"iati trydtsiaty," and others, who apparently manifests full sympathy for the Ukrainian national cause, subsequently reneges on this position and switches to full support for an opposite stance, to Bolshevism. The first difficulty with this argument is that Tychyna's purported "nationalism" is never defined or elaborated — it is always much bigger and more general than, indeed transcendent to, any political orientation. The concluding lines from *Zamist' sonetiv i oktav* (a work which, nota bene, is still censored by the Soviets and highly esteemed by émigré critics) sum up this "nationalism":

> Орел, Тризубець, Серп і Молот... І кожне виступає як своє
> Своєж рушниця в нас убила.
> Своє на дні душі лежить.

(The already cited final line which follows — "Khiba i sobi potsiluvat' pantofliu Papy?" — should thus be seen as referring not just to the "red" Pope, but to the Popes of all of the competing political dogmas.) It should be added, moreover, that Tychyna's espousal of Communist doctrine or the Party line in the late poetry is also frequently eminently superficial, in that it is populist or "folk-utopian," or ambivalent, or distanced (the device of presenting the vox populi not the voice of the poet in *Chernihiv* or *Partiia vede*). One must again repeat that in the case of Tychyna even an ode to Lenin or Stalin is not a political statement. The second difficulty is one of establishing periods: if the "break" is fundamentally political, and if it then occasions the inevitable qualitative change, then one is still at a loss to determine when precisely this occurs. Certainly not in *Pluh* or *Viter z Ukraïny,* which contain some of Tychyna's best poetry, nor in the complex and experimental and aesthetically valuable *Chernihiv,* nor even in *Partiia vede,* which also presents a number of artistically successful poems. I would argue that the question for the critic should be the moment when *a collection, a book of poems, as a semantic unit,* becomes unidimensional and circumscribed, and this occurs quite late, in the forties and later. At the same time, however, this one-sidedness is "compensated" by a sizeable body of poetry written not for publication — and to this we shall return. Finally, still speaking of the overt "political" level, the "surrender" to the Party does not come suddenly with *Partiia vede* in 1933; it is, at the very least, a gradual and continuous process that begins with the psychodrama "Rozkol poetiv" written in 1919. And what is involved is not a discrete moment, a "surrender," but the process of accepting a new reality, which is a Communist reality.

Another aspect of the surface or manifest level is that of thematics. Here the most evident development is a shift from the dominance of the natural setting in the earliest poetry and in *Soniashni kliarnety* (and partially in *Pluh*) to an urban, industrial setting in *Viter z Ukraïny* and *Chernihiv;* yet this does not entail any lowering of aesthetic achievement. Such a lowering and diluting and hence a form of aesthetic discontinuity does occur, however, when in the later poetry, partially of the late thirties, but especially the forties and fifties, the themes are strictly circumscribed and prescribed. When, for example, an ostensibly lyrical love poem ("Nad Dniprom," 1955), patterned after a well-known folk song, has not only the setting of two lovers by the water on a starry night but also such additional elements as the information that he is Ukrainian and she is Russian and that the city in the distance is one that they both defended during the war and that they will go off at daybreak to build a new future — then these elements can indeed be seen as a discordant imposition vitiating the poem.

Closely connected to this thematic change is the shift from pure lyricism to other stances — to the poet as tribune, as pedagogue, agitator and propagandist, in a word, as Trotskii would have it, as "engineer of the human soul." But this is a far more complex issue than the one of imposed themes. For even a cursory reading will show that from the very beginning, from the pre-*Soniashni kliarnety* poetry, and then the early collections, to the very end, Tychyna's poetry is dominated and determined precisely by the dichotomy of the poet as lyrical ego and the poet as tribune and spokesman for the collective, for his nation. This constitutes a central structure of his work, and in this regard there is full continuity. The change that does occur is gradual and it consists of a narrowing of his horizons and rights so that instead of a genuine tribune who draws his authority from his deep resonance with the nation he becomes an official spokesman whose authority, and indeed right to exist can come only from the Party. The two termini are indeed extreme opposites, but the road between them is one of gradual, not abrupt change. But there is also, as I have noted, at least a partial compensation, which is the retreat into a private lyrical poetry that was not included in any collection and only appeared posthumously, and which remained to some extent quite free of official notes and required themes. (It now constitutes a sizeable portion of the most recent, two-volume edition of his poetry.[6]) In short, this poetry testifies that even if he did not publish, Tychyna the true lyrical poet did not disappear.

The second level, that of formal aspects, is as broad as it is important, and it can hardly be fully examined here; I can only point to some central issues. One of these is an evolution in the matter of genre. The lyric mode, as I have noted, does continue, even as it becomes severely truncated. There is, however, growth and significant elaboration in the dramatic mode. From the very beginning, as in "Dzvinkoblakytne," "Rozkol poetiv," the collection *Zamist' sonetiv i oktav,* and in various individual poems, the dramatic element — as the basic constructive principle, as epiphany, or as contrasting interlude — is central for Tychyna. In the later poetry, already in the fragment called "Chystyla maty kartopliu," and then in such longer works as, for example, "Shablia Kotovs'koho" (1938) and "Shevchenko i Chernyshevs'kyi" (1939) it becomes even more pronounced. Its most successful artistic incarnation occurs in conjunction with Tychyna's ever present fascination for the musical construction, that is, in the "oratorio" *Chernihiv* and the "symphony" *Skovoroda*. At the same time, in the later poetry, Tychyna puts ever greater emphasis on the longer narrative *poema;* this is not always successful, and the underlying search for the epic note — which clearly was not organic to Tychyna — would seem to reflect the official desiderata of monumental style. Rather more interesting — as a direct counterbalance to the forced impoverishment of the lyrical voice — is Tychyna's cultivation of various subgenres of the "collective lyric," the group song, the ode, the paean and encomium, in short, the whole gamut of songs of work, praise and imprecation. Again, the crucial structure here, emblematically revealed in *Chernihiv* and *Partiia vede,* is that the authorial source is not the individual but the collective, not the voice of the poet but the vox populi.

Perhaps the most important formal consideration for us is the change in Tychyna's poetic style. The difference between the early *Soniashni kliarnety* and the poetry of his later collection is extreme and seems to point to a radical discontinuity. It is most instructive, for example, to compare the poetic credos ("grammars of themes"), given in "Tsvit v moiemu sertsi" (*Soniashni kliarnety*) on the one hand,

Цвіт в моєму серці,
Ясний цвіт-первоцвіт,
Ти той цвіт, мій друже,
Срібляний первоцвіт.
Ах, ізнов, кохана,
Де звучала рана —
Квітне цвіт-первоцвіт!

> Слухаю мелодій
> Хмар, озер та вітру.
> Я бриню, як струни
> Степу, хмар та вітру.
> Всі ми серцем дзвоним,
> Сним вином червоним —
> Сонця, хмар та вітру! . . .

and the opening strophes of "Stara Ukraïna zminytys' musyt'" (*Chernihiv*) on the other,

> Перекочовуючи насичуючись
> кількісно якісно перехлюпуючись
> проймаючи взаємно протилежності
> запереченням старого вибухаючи
> прямуєм за законом діялектики
> до н е з м і р é н н о г о майбутнього
>
> Отже перепони всі досліджено
> отже глибини всі розгадано
> отже з'ясовано всі недомудрення
> Розженімось цюкнім по історії
> може одкришиться нам ви́ломок
> од н е з в и ч а й н о г о майбутнього. . .

In summary fashion one could say that the early poetry's dominant impressionism (pointillism), the focus on the detail that is lit from within by a corresponding idea and emotion, is supplanted by large rhetorical and ultimately abstract formulations. Tychyna's early symbolic system, based on traditional, folk, and personal associations, on an oscillation between reality and revery, on synesthesia, and a blurring of the cosmos and the self, is subordinated to the normative. In the later poetry there is a marked flattening, or even total deletion of ambiguity, plurisignification or "nedoskazannist'." At the same time, Tychyna's concern for formal complexity is not easily or suddenly surrendered: between the two poles there are a number of intervening artistically valuable formal variations, for example the constructivist aspect of *Chernihiv,* the traditional folk-bouffe elements of "Shablia Kotovs'koho" or *Skovoroda,* and so on.[7] The shift in poetics is significant, but it does not imply a lowering of aesthetic quality; on the contrary, it shows remarkable formal sophistication.

The final level, that of deeper structures, is the most fundamental. That level entails the very self-definition of the poet and his psychocultural values. Since a fuller analysis cannot be attempted here, I merely wish to note that the innermost core of the deep structure is, quite simply, the imperative of consonance. The deep structure has various hypostases, but they all reveal the same principle: in *Soniashni kliarnety* (so programmatically expressed in the title poem) the need for consonance is manifest in a pantheistic sense of union with the Supreme Being, the cosmos itself; in this and the following three collections that need dictates the stance of the poet as the heart, the conscience and the voice of his people; in the subsequent poetry, with the lyrical ego now bracketed, consonance suggests the role of the poet as spokesman, who, even though he is an official spokesman, has legitimacy because he has experienced what the people have experienced, and indeed because he has sacrificed his personal voice for the common voice. In that sense, his surrender is not to the Party but to reality, and this is consonant with the precept voiced in *Skovoroda* — "Na vsikh shliakhakh . . . iednai svoiu khystkuiu voliu z voleiu tvortsia."[8]

It must be stressed that this structure is not to be conceived simplistically or reductively; it involves a fundamental tension and dialectic between personality and impersonality, as summarized by the formula-motto of *Soniashni kliarnety:* "Ia buv — ne Ia"; it involves agonizing self-questioning and self-restructuring as we see from his most intimate projection of himself as poet — in the impressive diary-confession-exorcism that is his *Skovoroda.* Nor is it a merely emotionally held principle, whereby we can claim, as some have done, that Tychyna perceives and writes subliminally, and functions like a great collective tympanum. On the contrary, in much of his poetry, if certainly not in all, the quest is also intellectual and ethical — as evidenced by his chosen models of Orpheus and Skovoroda — and also artistic, as seen in the formal searchings of his poetry.

The import of my overview is straightforward. The complexity of Tychyna's poetry taken as a system is too evident to submit it to simplistic and sectarian interpretations. It reveals far-reaching changes, but changes that are part of a larger, evolving, internally compensating process. Despite the transformations and notwithstanding unevenness in quality, the core of that process remains stable and coherent. It is time, it would seem, that the thoughtful critic would recognize that Tychyna, young or old, is one.

Harvard University

NOTES

1. "Literaturnyi shliakh Maksyma Ryl's'koho (1910 – 1925)," *Do dzherel* (Cracow, 1943), p. 239.
2. Ievhen Malaniuk, *Knyha sposterezhen'* (Toronto, 1962), vol. 1, p. 302.
3. Ivan Koshelivets', *Suchasna literatura v URSR* (New York, 1964), p. 85.
  Vasyl' Barka, *Khliborobs'kyi orfei, abo kliarnetyzm* (Munich, 1961), p. 87.
5. See my "A Decade of Tyčyniana," *Harvard Ukrainian Studies,* vol. 2, no. 1 (March, 1978), pp. 119-29.
6. Pavlo Tychyna, *Tvory,* ed. O.I. Kudin (2 vols.; Kiev, 1976).
7. See my "Tyčyna's *Černihiv,*" *Harvard Ukrainian Studies,* vol. 1, no. 1 (March, 1977), pp. 79-113.
8. Pavlo Tychyna, *Skovoroda: Symfoniia* (Kiev, 1971), p. 54.

ALL OF ALIJA'S WOMEN:
ANDRIĆ'S REALIZATION OF 'EX PONTO' VISIONS

ŽELIMIR JURIČIĆ

The Journey of Đerzelez Alija (*Put Alije Đerzeleza*, 1920),[1] marks a turning point in Andrić's literary career. This work is his first short story, the genre in which he eventually established himself as a major Yugoslav writer and attained international stature. It was the first work which he set in Bosnia, the land where he was born and schooled. Bosnia, with its exotic character, was to Andrić "the most interesting country in Europe,"[2] a well of information and inspiration. Her colorful inhabitants, Moslems, Roman Catholics, Sephardic Jews, Orthodox Christians, and Turks (both the ethnic and converted), provided Andrić with a rich pool of literary characters. Throughout his career Andrić remained true to his native region and he attained eminence as Bosnia's most recognized chronicler.

More importantly, *The Journey* marks Andrić's departure from the subjective tone of his early writings, including two volumes of poetic prose, *Ex Ponto*, 1918, and *Disquiet (Nemiri)*, 1920, and a number of lyrics, for the harsh, somberly realistic rendition of his experiences through the depiction of others. His new idiom and subject matter were so different, that Isidora Sekulić, a veteran writer and an intelligent observer of the contemporary literary scene, found it "difficult to believe that the Andrić of the short stories is the same man who wrote the delicate, sentimental, Christian, and typically Western *Ex Ponto* and *Disquiet*."[3]

Aside from the writer's sudden shift from poetry to prose, from the sentimental and inquisitive to a realistic style, and despite his obviously greater maturity, no doubt a result of his three-year internment (1914 – 1917) under the Austrians, a number of structural and contextual similarities suggest that *Ex Ponto* and *The Journey* form a natural link in Andrić's development. *The Journey* is a natural outgrowth of *Ex Ponto*, its reflection in prose. Many views on life and existence which are characteristic of his poetry, as well as a directness of language and style, permeate also his narrative prose.

In structure, both *Ex Ponto* and *The Journey* are trilogies. Partially written during Andrić's internment, the three distinct yet uneven parts and the page-long Epilogue of *Ex Ponto* were published as a book in 1918. In the same year the literary journal *Književni Jug*, of which the young Andrić was one of the editors and founders, published the first part of *The Journey, Đerzelez at the Khan*. The second part of the trilogy, *Đerzelez on the Road,* was published in the same journal a year later, and the third, *Đerzelez in Sarajevo,* was published in 1920, when the entire narrative was also published.

It is possible that during the process of conception and during the actual writing, the author might have worked on both pieces simultaneously, and that a degree of osmosis of ideas inevitably occurred. Many of the philosophical ideas which Andrić put into *The Journey* can be found to have originated, mostly under the guise of personal experiences and visions, in *Ex Ponto*. The subject of women, which is central to both works, and indeed to Andrić's entire mosaic of existence, is a good example.

Either as man's companion, as an object of beauty and admiration, or as an evil force in his life, woman influences every aspect of man's life. Be he friar or thief, wise or foolish, no man can escape being affected by her. "She stands like a gate both at the exit as well as the entrance of this world."[4] To the young Andrić woman was always a profound secret, an enigma, whose mysterious psyche he was unable to fathom. All his attempts ended in pain and misery:

> Why can we not see you clearly as our ancestors saw you in the sun, but you have become a frightened vision and a poison in our blood; we run before you and when we think we have lost you, you keep vigil in our thoughts. When, by working, we try to forget you — look — on all our exploits thin lines, wind, the traces of your unseen fingers. What is the meaning of the undulating line of your body? And of your reticent, white, widely sung beauty which we restlessly pursue, like children the butterfly, but which either gives us pain or transforms itself into bitterness?[5]

"Night, in particular," wrote Andrić in *Ex Ponto,* "was always an evil time in my life. When the soul is asleep like a dead stone at the bottom of the sea, women appear to me in fantastic shapes and sizes." (*Ex Ponto,* p. 50.) They represent happiness and love, a world of logic and peace which man is desperately trying to reach but cannot because of personal, social, or moral obstacles. This unrealizable yearning for the inaccessible is visualized in *Ex Ponto* as a meeting between a writer and the dream woman called the "nepomućena radost života" ("an undisturbed joy of life"), which never takes place:

> I arrived. She did not. I waited for her. At first I waited patiently and expectantly, and then even more anxiously and solemnly. Hours went by . . . and my waiting passed into despair . . . she never came. A terrible woman. I think she finds pleasure in someone else's misery. She arranges meetings with hundreds of people simultaneously and while they wait on a hundred corners, looking pained as if holding live coals in their intestines, she stands, somewhere, at the edge of the city, behind the window, and with a resigned face stiffly watches the fields being engulfed in darkness (p. 62).

Besides their physical attractiveness, Andrić's women in *Ex Ponto* frequently represent an ideal, an inaccessible world diametrically opposed to the one in which men are condemned to live and suffer. There is no reconciliation between the two worlds — the night woman keeps on walking the corridors of the writer's mind, immune to his wishes:

> I always see you as you stumble while walking furtively along the

half-lit corridor with a light in your hand towards the door, but you never cross the threshold. My whole soul trembles like a light in your hand, but you can neither come nor return; you are roaming forever in the dark corridor (p. 77).

Andrić's visions of women both as representative of an imagined reality to which men turn out of despondency and desperation, as flashes of sporadic happiness amidst the evil of life, and as the perpetual tormentors of passionate personalities, are again realized in *The Journey*. However, in order to express experience outside his own lyrical sphere, Andrić changed both the stage and cast for the narrative.

The author's prison cell, in which much of *Ex Ponto* was written, is replaced in *The Journey* by Bosnia, a remote border province of the Ottoman Empire, a barren and desolate land. In place of the many nameless apparitions, shadows, and visions (only one woman, Jelena, is referred to by name in *Ex Ponto*),[6] which hazily appear *to the author* in perpetually alternating patterns, particularly by night — real flesh and blood women, with names, or some qualifying apellations, populate *The Journey*, for example, Zemka, Katinka, Ivka, Ekaterina, a woman from Venice, a fat widow, and a devious Jewess. Appending labels to both animate and inanimate objects is another sign of the author's conscious effort to shift from a personal to a public reality where everything and everyone has a designation and place. The hero of Andrić's first short story is regarded as the greatest hero of his race, the colorful legendary warrior of Bosnian-Moslem epics — Đerzelez Alija. Endowed with a robust vitality, immense strength, and an enviable appearance, Đerzelez is one of those powerful characters which rise from the depths of legend to visit the unhappy present. By examining life through his hero's experiences as he travels through Bosnia, the author deliberately accentuates the "objective" in the narrative.

From the outset of the story it is evident that Đerzelez is hardly an incarnation of the heroism and spiritual harmony of the legend. In Bosnia, a land of cunning and deceit, his strength is a detriment to him, and women are his Achilles heel. The hero's subjugation of everything to an insatiable sexual drive only underscores the frustration of his strong personality. In the course of his exploits Đerzelez encounters six women (this excludes the passing appearance of Ivka Grguša, a tall and burly old crone of a matchmaker who plays only a peripheral role in the story). They can be divided into two equal groups, the ideal women, who correspond to Andrić's dream women in *Ex Ponto,* and the women of reality who, as will be seen below, also originate there. Đerzelez encounters first the ideal group, including a Venetian woman, the gypsy Zemka, and Katinka. To the second group belong a Jewess, a fat widow, and the prostitute Ekaterina.

Typically for Andrić, there is no room in his narrative for deep psychological sounding, or full-blown canvases of his heroines: a few strokes of the pen, as if for a sketch, is the extent of his description. For example, there is "the slender Venetian in her wide skirt of green velvet and her small head above the fur collar,"[7] or the folkloristic portrayal of the gypsy Zemka, "the barefaced and crafty yet also loving animal" (*The Journey,* p. 42). And finally, Katinka, "a girl in light pantaloons and a red waistcoat, so young and full like a bunch of grapes" (p. 35). Like most of Andrić's women, be they real or imagined, they are exceptionally beautiful. The Venetian woman's body "slender and aristocratic, was past imagining" (p. 42). Zemka, "with her green eyes and slender figure, was fairer than all other gypsies" (p. 27). And Katinka had a "pale, lean face, luxuriant hair, and an ample, lush body" (p. 40). Although Đerzelez sees them only from a distance, either on the top of the stairway (the Venetian woman), on a swing (Zemka), or in the courtyard (Katinka), and somewhat blurred and sketchy, as if "through misty eyes" (p. 22), or "as in a dream" (p. 23), his whole being is shaken at the sight of them. Something powerful, mysteriously intoxicating, like a tidal wave from deep within him, engulfs him and makes him lose his balance. "He tingled all over with a tingle that was now cold, now in his very loins" (p. 29). "Always when he came face to face with womanly beauty, he at once lost all sense of time and proportion, as well as all understanding of the reality that separated people one from another" (p. 35).

The outward signs of Đerzelez' disquiet are his heavy perspiring, excessive drinking and smoking, and even the duel into which he is easily enticed by a knife peddler from Foča, a perverse individual. Đerzelez seems to be much better at "making his point with his hands than with his words" (p. 19). However, both in the field of battle and in the woman's boudoir, he ends up a loser. The duel turns out to be nothing more than a practical joke, which settles nothing and makes him out a fool, a pathetic, wretched soul. Strength appears ridiculous in the midst of the petty life of these Bosnian folk who are always ready for cunning and deceit. He fares no better in his erotic escapades. What seems to him to be an easy world to conquer — "he never for an instant doubted his rights; all he had to do was to stretch out his hand" (p. 35) — turned out to be just beyond his reach; he finds all the doors to women's hearts padlocked, "as if under a curse" (p. 40). The Venetian woman manages to vanish in front of his very eyes, "behind the door of her room, followed by a loud click" (p. 22). And when he attempts to corner Zemka "she suddenly wheeled left and vanished, as in a dream" (p. 32). And Katinka, about whose beauty songs are sung all over Bosnia, also, is "gone! Gone!" (p. 39) before he can come even close to her. Thus, vacillating between an evil reality, which he can neither understand nor endure, and a visionary paradise (symbolized by the ideal woman) closed to him, the fever-driven, soul-tormented, overly sensuous hero ends up grotesquely misunderstood and miserable. "Was this some kind of game? Were they using him as a fool? What sort of joke was this again? What sort of women were these that you couldn't get hold of, as if they were God?" (p. 40). Unfortunate, glorious, and foolish, unable despite his fame, strength, and his good sword to enter the world of beauty, Đerzelez *temporarily* abandons his quest of the ideal and goes on living the best he can in the existing world. Despite his firm resolution "never again to have near him anything female — not even a cat, not even a cat!" (p. 29), he easily succumbs to his sensual craving for female flesh by visiting the "women of reality."

If the road to the "ideal women" is enigmatic, tortuous, and futile, the road to the women of the lower levels of life is not. They give their love freely, or for a price, asking for no promises and making no demands. They, too, have their origin in *Ex Ponto*. Like the ideal women, the women of reality are also beautiful and inviting. Unlike the former, they "open their pistils to all the winds," asking no questions, disturbing no man's mind (*Ex Ponto*, p. 32). Once, a vision of such a woman appeared to Andrić in *Ex Ponto:* he dreamed that he loved a beautiful sixteen-year-old girl, whose tongue he could scarcely understand, for one day only. However enticing, "one-day loves" in Andrić are rare, and of no lasting consequence. They seldom grow into more enduring relationships, for a pure, Dantean love is unknown to Andrić.

The worst of loves in *Ex Ponto* is that found in the bosom of a prostitute, in a boudoir laden with wine and music. Andrić relates the experience thus:

> I drank wine, red and heavy as misfortune. I walked as though poisoned. And when the wine overcame me I raged all night. The last thing I saw was in a large mirror: I was lying waxen-faced, and around me prostitutes, one holding my wallet and counting money. When I woke up — it was in a small garden — my dinner jacket was wet and my hands bloody from the broken glasses — bloody and naked (pp. 36 – 37).

The sexually frustrated Đerzelez finds comfort in the arms of three similar women: "the fat widow of a tradesman from Ušćup" (p. 33), "the passionate and devious Jewess who kept company with some musicians from Selnik" (pp. 33, 42), and Ekaterina, a prostitute. The first two are Đerzelez' "one-day loves," beings who are also unhappy and frustrated, being relegated to the bottom of life by a harsh and merciless reality with which they cannot negotiate. They and the hero find momentary comfort in each other's misery. Đerzelez finds Ekaterina, the prostitute, sitting "in a small and neat room, lighted softly by curtains of delicate white silk... with her placid eyes and white arms, as if waiting" (p. 41). Like those of her counterpart in *Ex Ponto,* her doors are always open to her good and old customers. "She was the only one a man reached in a straight line" (p. 42). To Đerzelez, however, Ekaterina's tiny and gentle hand, caressing him deftly and expertly up and down the spine, the fat widow's and the devious Jewess' comforting moments, are but a "short pause before he resumes his journey" (p. 43). There are Katinkas, Zemkas, and Venetian women waiting to be conquered; and Ekaterinas will be waiting to cushion his fall every time he descends from his imaginary paradise back to reality. The search for satisfaction and fulfillment is irrepressible in him.

Although in his mature works Andrić concentrated more on pain, suffering, hatred, isolation, and fear, on all that is vicious in the world, the subject of women and their effect on men — as first envisioned in *Ex Ponto* and realized in *The Journey* — continued to occupy his mind as one of the important facets of his study of men and their fates. In fact, "all Andrić's later stories about women trace their ancestry to *The Journey*,"[8] and many of Đerzelez' descendants, such as Ćorkan (*Ćorkan and the German Women,* 1921), Mustafa Madžar (*Mustafa Madžar,* 1923) and Professor V (*The Signs,* 1951), also fall victim to the forces of love and to women who are just as mysterious and destructive. A warning to everyone and an object of ridicule in his ventures to conquer a member of the opposite sex, Đerzelez is not merely a Bosnian braggart, but a symbol of man in general confronted by the eternal problem presented by woman.

In Andrić's narrative art, women play a dual role. They are a symbol of physical beauty which exercises a magnetic influence over men. Like an unseen worm, they destroy slowly from within, and there is no remedy against this cancerous malady. They also symbolize another world which men may glimpse and yearn for but are unable to reach. The desire for the inaccessible and the beautiful, particularly when pursued by physically strong, but overly sensuous and erotically vulnerable individuals, is almost always coupled with the delusion of its attainment. "I have seen that this life is a painful affair which consists of sin and misery, that to live means to pile illusion upon illusion," wrote Andrić in *Ex Ponto* (p. 101).

Ex Ponto and *The Journey*, like many of Andrić's other writings, are permeated with a feeling of sadness and doom. Everything appears futile in view of the ubiquitous presence of death, uselessness, and emptiness. Andrić's imprisonment, his reading of Dostoevsky, Kierkegaard, and the works of the medieval Bogomils may have contributed somewhat to this fatalistic pessimism, which has continued to mark his work. But there is another side to Andrić's concept of love, women, and, indeed, existence. Life is a constant struggle between the opposites of nature, especially in the human soul. Ubiquitous enmities and contradictions may, and often do, lead to individual tragedies but not to an unequivocal denial of life. Life is still stronger than the forces which threaten its destruction. This aspect of Andrić's philosophy transcends the real and the obvious and elevates his view of human existence to the level of universality.

> On the one hand — the desire to find a way out and to escape at all costs from this life into the freedom of nonexistence which constantly calls us and draws us towards itself with great strength. On the other hand — instinctive love for life and a constant yearning to exist here and last forever. These two things only appear to be irreconcilable and contradictory. And I am one of those who, from his first movement in his mother's womb to the very last moment, is always looking for a way out.[9]

University of Victoria

NOTES

1. Henceforth referred to as *The Journey*.
2. Ljubo Jandrić, *Sa Ivom Andrićem* (Belgrade: Srpska Književna Zadruga, 1977), p. 275.
3. Isidora Sekulić, "Istok u pripovetkama Iva Andrića," *Kritičari o Andriću*, ed. Petar Džadžić (Belgrade: Nolit, 1962), p. 58.

4. Ivo Andrić, "Smrt u Sinanovoj Tekiji," *Žeđ* (Sarajevo: Svjetlost, 1977), p. 212.

5. Ivo Andrić, *Ex Ponto* (Zagreb: Književni Jug, 1917), p. 43. This and the following translations from *Ex Ponto* are mine.

6. See Želimir Juričić, "Andrić's Vision of Women in 'Ex Ponto'," *Slavic and East European Journal,* vol. 23, no. 2 (1979), pp. 233–39.

7. Ivo Andrić, "The Journey of Ali Djerzelez," *The Pasha's Concubine and other Tales,* tr. Joseph Hitrec (New York: Alfred Knopf, 1968), p. 27.

8. Stanko Korač, "Žena u Andrićevim pripovetkama," *Zbornik radova o Ivi Andriću* (Belgrade: Srpska Akademija Nauka i Umjetnosti, 1979), Book 30, p. 555.

9. Ivo Andrić, *Znakovi pored puta* (Sarajevo: Svjetlost, 1978), pp. 110, 113 (my translation).

THE CONTEMPORARY POLISH HISTORICAL NOVEL AND ITS POLITICAL INSPIRATIONS

JERZY R. KRZYŻANOWSKI

The title of this paper indicates more than meets the eye: certain methodological problems must be considered before we can discuss the political inspirations of the contemporary Polish historical novel. Because Polish literary scholars have applied some literary terms superficially and mechanically, without any insight into their semantic and logical implications, we must first clarify some basic questions before we can address the second part of this paper's title.

What, exactly, is a "contemporary" novel? A novel written in the last twenty years? Or after World War II, that is, in the last thirty-five years? Considering the massive changes in the political and social situation, and the lasting results of the war, one is inclined to propose the use of the latter definition, for there is a unity in postwar literature which sets it sharply aside from anything written in the prewar period.

The second term, "Polish," will be applied not only to novels written in Poland, for there is a unity in Polish literature, whether it be written and published in Poland, or published abroad for political reasons, or even written and published in any one of a dozen foreign countries where Polish writers live. Although Polish émigré writers have not contributed significantly — with only a few exceptions — to the creation of contemporary historical novels, their works should be considered a vital part of Polish literature, even when they choose to write in languages other than Polish.

The third definition, "historical," is perhaps the most complicated to establish and not only in the context of Polish literature. The major Polish historical novelists, J.I. Kraszewski and H. Sienkiewicz, whose works introduced that genre more than a hundred years ago, set their novels in eras quite remote from their own lifetimes. Sienkiewicz's trilogy goes back in time some 250 years, his *Teutonic Knights* some 500 years, and his renowned best seller *Quo vadis?* almost 2000 years, to the beginning of Christianity. Kraszewski shortened the time span between his own epoch and the time setting of his novels — in *Saskie ostatki* (1889) he presented events of only a hundred years before. In his recently published memoir *Kurier z Warszawy* J. Nowak recalls:

> Since my early childhood I was taught to take off my hat in front of a veteran of the 1863 uprising. Some of them, such as Aleksander Kraushar, Bolesław Limanowski or Siehen I knew by sight. Once, during a visit at our friends, my mother pointed out to me a ninety-year-old man with a magnificent, long, gray beard, and whispered in my ear: "Remember, son, Mr. Rudomina-Dusiacki was a commander of a party during the uprising in Lithuania."[1]

Many Polish writers share Nowak's experience, for he represents a middle-age generation, junior to a number of still active authors. How far then must a writer go back in order to break away from memories still alive and establish the perspective necessary to create a dispassionate, objective, historical novel? J. Krzyżanowski in his study *Nauka o literaturze* proposes a simple definition:

> The simplest method is the time of the novel's action measured against the writer's time: when the novel's action takes place before his epoch, in a chronologically determined milieu, we call it a historical novel.[2]

But, at the same time, he gives a long list of variants, such as "historical-adventure novel," "sociohistorical," "psychological-historical," etc., depending on the predominant elements in the novel. As far as the definition of the historical novel is concerned, he clearly uses the concept of generations in its biological and social rather than literary sense. It should not be confused with the term "literary generation," coined by H. Peyre in his study *Les Generations littéraires* (1948) and more recently expanded by K. Wyka in his study *Pokolenia literackie* (1977). Both studies emphasize the coexistence of several generations of writers working in the same epoch and gradually replacing each other in an unbroken "changing of the guard," as the Polish critic J. Błoński aptly called the process.

For the purpose of defining the term "historical" however the distance between generations is more important than their coexistence. The problem is further complicated by the political and social changes occurring in the lifetime of each generation. The circumstances before World War II and those after it are so different that, in spite of the continuity of literary life, it would be almost impossible to compare the two images as perceived by literature. For the generation of writers born in postwar Poland, everything that existed before the war has the ring almost of ancient history and is yet too close in time and heritage to be viewed as such. It is the psychological distance between the generations which separates them and it affects even those writers who began writing in the prewar period. It seems necessary for a writer to extricate himself from the web of factors affecting his perception and vision, and to go back in history without losing touch with the present, to write a historical novel which would be meaningful for his own generation. In the case of Poland there appears to exist a convenient historical juncture which meets these requirements, a juncture remote by a hundred years and yet as vivid and meaningful as any event in more recent history, namely the 1863 uprising. And for this reason one is inclined to propose here the following working definition of the term "historical" novel: one whose action takes place at least one hundred years before its publication or, to be more precise, refers to the events of 1863 at the latest.

These attempts to define more precisely the terminology of literary studies deliberately omit another set of major theoretical problems, such as the question of time in a novel's structure, but there seems to be a rather urgent need to make literary terminology more precise. S. Skwarczyńska, in her study of literary genres *Wstęp do nauki o literaturze,* which is based on the most recent Polish and foreign discussions of the problem, demonstrated quite clearly that there exists a rather widespread confusion about theoretical definitions.[3] More and more scholars are involved in structural studies of intrinsic problems in literary texts, but only a few seem to feel the need for a broad synthesis which, in turn, would necessitate a precise terminology. Dictionaries of literary terms and popular attempts at literary theory such as *Zarys teorii literatury* by M. Głowiński, A. Okopień-Sławińska, and J. Sławiński, published in 1967 by PZWS, a publisher of high school textbooks in Poland, do not solve the problem but add to the confusion.

In the narrow field of the historical novel, these problems have preoccupied writers and scholars throughout the world, from Goethe to Henry James, and from Belinskii to Warren and Wellek. Scholars pay considerable attention to the question of the historical novel as a genre, but the novelists seem to be less concerned with its theoretical implications and define it in their own practical terms. Sienkiewicz, defending his historical trilogy against attacks by positivistic critics, stated simply that "there are no bad or good trends — there are only those which at a given time must exist, those created by life."[4] And he continued: "The historical novel does not have to abuse the truth, either life's truth or historical truth. It can be as real and pulsate with as much life as any [novel] based on contemporary conditions."[5] He declared his freedom to write on historical topics during a period of preoccupation with contemporary issues and he defended the historical novel as a major artistic, social, and psychological achievement in modern fiction.

There are other problems relating to the genre of the historical novel. One is the novelist's choice to emphasize either the historical personages who predominate in the plot or the fictitious characters who carry the action. Another, rather infrequent device is the replacement of real names with fictitious ones, as is the case in an American novel on the Warsaw Ghetto, *The Wall* by John Hersey. In the Polish tradition, the discussion of this question dates back to a dispute between the critic M. Grabowski and the novelist Kraszewski. While Grabowski advocated Walter Scott's practice of emphasizing the fictitious characters, Kraszewski gave more attention to historical figures in a manner which later, particularly at the turn of the century, developed into the *vie romancée* genre and fictionalized biographies of real persons.[6]

Another theoretical problem brought up recently by Polish scholars is the importance of literary work as a historical source, as demonstrated in a collection of essays, *Dzieło literackie jako źródło historyczne*.[7] Given the tremendous impact historical novels have in forming the image of the past, further research should be undertaken not only by literary scholars but by sociologists, historians, educators and even psychologists, which would indicate the responsibility of the novelist on the one hand, and the attitudes of the reading public on the other, and add to a sense of the importance of the historical novel.

For the time being, however, these methodological remarks must be concluded with working definitions of the terms used in the title of this paper: "contemporary" refers to novels written and published between 1945 and 1980; "Polish" means works written by Polish authors without regard to geographical or even language restrictions; "historical" includes only novels whose subject matters do not go beyond the events of the 1863 uprising, thus removing the author at least three biological generations from his topic; and finally "novel" indicates works of fiction rather than the fictionalized biographies of *vie romancées*.

*

The task of surveying the contemporary Polish historical novel has been challenging. In the period under discussion some 8,000 titles of new fiction were published by Polish authors in Poland and abroad. Out of these roughly half were novels, but historical novels represent only some four percent of the total, that is, some 150 titles. Clearly the writers are preoccupied either with contemporary topics or with the more recent past, with World War II emerging as perhaps the most fascinating, and certainly the predominant, theme. But only some fifty titles meet high literary standards and thus deserve to be discussed as important contributions to the field of the historical novel. The remainder can be designated as "not a work of art but a literary substitute," *Ersatzliteratur,* as the Polish critic A. Kijowski described it.[8] Also dismissed are a number of the *vie romancée* type of novel devoted to various hastily recreated revolutionary figures in Poland's history, such as Walery Wróblewski or Jarosław Dąbrowski. These novels are attempts to create the kind of Marxist hagiography so immensely popular in the Soviet Union and introduced to Polish letters particularly during the Socialist-Realist period of 1949-55.

High standards of artistic excellence were established by Kraszewski, Sienkiewicz, and Żeromski by the end of the nineteenth century, and their criteria still apply in the modern period, for one has to remember that their novels enjoy continuous popular appeal, inspiring not only literary works but also derivative forms such as motion pictures, TV series, and even comic books. The link between the nineteenth-century historical novel and modern literature remains unbroken, and certain patterns of that continuity can be easily discovered.

Kraszewski wrote his impressive cycle of historical novels in order to provide the nation, during the darkest period of Russian domination after the collapse of the 1863 uprising, with a set of records of Poland's tradition of greatness. Equally well-known is Sienkiewicz's goal "to uplift human hearts" with his historical trilogy in the age of positivistic, materialistically oriented ideology. But their novels performed yet another function, providing readers with a psychological escape from hard political realities, an escape contemporary novels could not have offered because of the sensitivity of some issues. In Poland's most realistic novel of that period, Prus's *The Doll* (1890), the author could only allude to his protagonist's patriotic deeds during the uprising while presenting the contemporary scene with such caution that only a close linguistic analysis might have disclosed that Warsaw in Prus's novel was under the Russian occupation.[9]

More or less the same escape mechanism is still used today, in postwar Poland. In 1972, in a paper presented at a panel on the literature of People's Poland, organized by the Jagiellonian University and the Institute of Literary Research of the Polish Academy of Sciences in Cracow, J. Błoński bluntly stated:

> But pondering upon what it is to be Polish has never been more popular than today. The only thing is, it has escaped into the past in Zawieyski's or Kuncewiczowa's [novels], into a past grotesquely unreal in Brandys', into a pure grotesque in Mrożek's or parodistic fable in Kijowski's. Detached from today's reality, the fables, the legends, and the Polish myths flourish at their best.[10]

And indeed, the past provided many authors with an ideal escape from the drab dogma of Socialist Realism in the 1950s, serving for some novelists as a forum where they could manifest their ideological and political credos. In the next two decades the historical novel offered to many authors a key to unlock the most crucial problems in the nation's collective consciousness, to search for the sources of the national ethos, to better understand the contemporary situation. The fact that a nonfictional cycle of historical essays, *Koniec świata szwoleżerów* by M. Brandys, has become highly sought-after is quite relevant in this respect, because of its striking comparison of the post-Napoleonic era and the problems former military heroes faced in Poland occupied by tsarist Russia to the similar situation the postwar generations have faced in Poland today.

Generally speaking the Polish historical novelists treat social problems and are ideologically motivated. Quite a few of them come from a strong Catholic community and are trying to explore in the past one of the most crucial problems in Poland's past and present history, the relationship between the Catholic Church and the State. A. Gołubiew's cycle of novels set in the eleventh century, at the very beginning of Poland's statehood, serve as a perfect example of such an interest.

On a broader scale, almost world-wide in scope, a similar problem is being treated in a most ambitious cycle of historical novels written by T. Parnicki. His fascination with the question of power is underscored by a recurring motif of investigation and official hearing ("śledztwo i przesłuchanie") leaving no doubt as to the author's views on the methods by which power is achieved and maintained. Although his political inspiration does not come from Catholic ideology, the theme of the power struggle between the Church and the State represents another major motif in his works.

The majority of Polish historical novelists belong to a rather skeptical, intellectually, but not necessarily spiritually, committed community of writers who feel obliged to use history as a tool for the better understanding of contemporary problems. They try, as a Polish critic M. Sprusiński put it, "to actualize historical sources making the experience of their characters timeless," but, at the same time, they "demythologize history," thus making it relevant to the contemporary reader.[11] This is a method common to novelists of all political and ideological persuasions. A Biblical novel was written by a Marxist author, H. Chmielewski, who used the story of Moses to present the thesis that "history is made by societies, not by Prophets."[12] The majority of Marxist novelists however are mostly limited by their ideological and artistic method, and their mass production of *Ersatzliteratur* prompted Sprusiński to paraphrase a well-known Marxist thesis stating that in their case "quantity turns into nothingness."[13]

The range of settings in the contemporary Polish historical novel is quite wide, from prehistoric and Biblical times up to 1863. The prevailing theme emerging seems to be the moral problem of responsibility for the national destiny, on both the personal and national levels. This theme, projected against that of the struggle for power, implies a strong moral judgment, for only those who are morally justified in controlling the national destiny are seen as right, while those who lack such a justification are usually condemned as usurpers and wrongdoers. That is, of course, a traditional approach, but there are also thinly veiled allusions to the political conditions in contemporary Poland, where the Communist Party controls the situation without being morally justified in doing so. Abuses of power, so frequent in history, are generally understood by the reading public as pertaining not so much to characters from the past as from the present.

Another recent phenomenon is an obvious emphasis on the national struggle for survival in armed encounters with Poland's external enemies. Poland's thousand-year history is a record of constant invasions, either from the West or from the East, and of the nation's defensive efforts to free itself from foreign influences and dominations. While war novels have been a traditional favorite with Polish authors, the most recent emphasis seems to be on uprisings against occupations, with 1863 emerging as a major topic. In a novel published in 1979 without official approval, T. Konwicki intertwines the events of 1863 with a contemporary plot, so that they become a pertinent motif in explaining "the Polish complex," as he titles his novel. When one keeps in mind that at the end of World War II the first novel republished after the Nazi occupation was Sienkiewicz's *Teutonic Knights,* as a manifestation of the national wrath against the Germans, this switch to an almost openly anti-Russian sentiment, emerging thirty-five years later, is quite indicative and self-explanatory.

The political inspiration of ideologies born at the turn of the century, such as socialism, national democracy, populism, etc., emerge in historical novels today with perhaps less strength than during the prewar era. They seem to be fading away somewhat under the pressure of the modern problems facing postwar society; nevertheless, they can be discerned in many historical novels. In some cases the authors try to use the motif of populism, the peasantry as a leading force, popular heroes, etc., to underscore their own political persuasion, but in recent years the balance seems to be restored as more and more historical novels bring back a rather nostalgic image of the monarchy, the aristocracy, and the nobility with their power, splendor, and traditional values. The Austro-Hungarian monarchy in particular emerges in A. Kuśniewicz's novels as a charming, fascinating country in which nationalities, social classes, and interest groups could coexist peacefully.

In general, one is tempted to see the contemporary Polish historical novel as an attempt to restore the sixteenth-century tradition of the "Golden Age" in Polish literature, with its tolerance of practically every creed and frame of mind, with its basically democratic spirit, and its freedom of expression, all permitted as long as they contributed to the national unity and the overall wellbeing of the country. Given more freedom of expression, the Polish historical novel would certainly develop along those lines and become as fascinating and inspiring as ever.

Ohio State University

NOTES

1. Jan Nowak, *Kurier z Warszawy* (London, 1978), p. 11.
2. Julian Krzyżanowski, *Nauka o literaturze* (Wroclaw, 1969), p. 215.
3. Stefania Skwarczyńska, *Wstęp do nauki o literaturze* (Warsaw, 1965), vol. 3, p. 344 ff.
4. Henryk Sienkiewicz, *Dzieła* (Warsaw, 1951), vol. 45, p. 104.
5. Ibid., p. 120.
6. See *Polska krytyka literacka (1800-1918)* (Warsaw, 1959), vol. 2, pp. 49-67, 97-99, 389-92, 408-13.
7. *Dzieło literackie jako źródło historyczne,* ed. Zofia Stefanowska and Janusz Sławiński (Warsaw, 1978).
8. *Rocznik literacki 1956* (Warsaw, 1957), p. 67.
9. See Ludwik B. Grzeniewski, *Warszawa v "Lalce" Prusa* (Warsaw, 1965.
10. *W kręgu literatury Polski Ludowej* (Cracow, 1975), p. 64.
11. *Rocznik literacki 1976* (Warsaw, 1979), p. 51.
12. Henryk Chmielewski, *Prorok* (Warsaw, 1971).
13. *Rocznik literacki 1972* (Warsaw, 1974), p. 72.

MYSTERIOUS AND IRRATIONAL ELEMENTS IN THE WORKS OF MYKHAILO KOTSIUBYNS'KYI AND THEODOR STORM

MYRON E. NOWOSAD

A certain amount of the mysterious and irrational is found in every period of literature and art. One can say that they are themselves the irrational spirit in a logical form. The intensity with which the mysterious and irrational are used greatly fluctuates, however, with the various periods of history. Mykhailo Kotsiubyns'kyi (1864-1913) and Theodor Storm (1817-1888) used the irrational to allude to actions which cannot be understood through reason. Kotsiubyns'kyi and Storm are illustrations, despite some current literary opinions, of the fact that the mysterious and irrational were still used extensively in European literature after the middle of the nineteenth century and even as late as the twentieth century.

The mysterious and irrational elements in the writings of Kotsiubyns'kyi have not as yet been analyzed. In the Communist world these elements are rejected, which may explain why Kotsiubyns'kyi critics have not dealt with this aspect of his work. However, neither did literary critics before the Communist take-over nor have those in exile examined these elements. By contrast with Kotsiubyns'kyi researchers, Storm researchers have occupied themselves for many years with the irrational and the mysterious. There are parallels between the two writers, and some comparisons can be made.

Kotsiubyns'kyi and Storm do not treat the mysterious and irrational consistently; the appearance in their works of inexplicable forces of nature or more sinister forces becomes more frequent during their later years. In their last completed works, Kotsiubyns'kyi's *Tini zabutykh predkiv* (Shadows of Forgotten Ancestors, 1912), and Storm's *Der Schimmelreiter* (1888), the sinister not only confronts the protagonists, but the protagonists themselves are the embodiment of the mysterious; even the frame of Storm's short story does not refute this impression unequivocally. The mysterious is seen as a force which helps to determine action. During the course of their writings, both authors again and again show inexplicable powers as influences on the conscious actions of men; at first these powers are indicated only by symbolic ambiguities in the external appearances of objects or creatures, as moods; but they become more tangible in the form of heredity, social environment, apparitions, spooks, or magic; and, finally, at the culmination of the author's creativity, man himself is shown as exposed to an environment dominated by demons and his own actions are determined by inexplicable forces. Fate, as it bears down on man from outside, as well as intrinsic human character, is influenced by factors which cannot be rationalized.

Besides the obviously irrational and mysterious elements in the works of both authors, there are occurrences which are depicted realistically, but which can be seen apart in such a way that the mysterious is clearly discernible. Most of these instances are descriptions of nature, but occasionally there are persons whose traits are described with such exaggeration that they become carriers of the irrational. Examples are the forest scene in *Immensee* (1852) and Hnat in *Na viru* (Concubinage, 1891). Beginning with *Shadows of Forgotten Ancestors* and *Der Schimmelreiter* similar elements can be detected.

Nature, animate as well as inanimate, for Kotsiubyns'kyi and Storm no longer remains a mere sounding-board for human emotions as had been the case with I. Nechui-Levyts'kyi (1838–1918) or G. Keller (1819–1890). With these other writers, nature and death were felt to be liberators and a way to peace, but Kotsiubyns'kyi and Storm experience in nature a fear of the strange, the inaccessible, and death. For both authors nature is no longer a refuge, rather it progressively acquires an intrinsic sinister force. In the authors' last works nature intervenes decisively in the life and fate of the protagonists. Ivan's and Hauke's desires for self-realization are not only ruined by Marichka's death in the river and by the animosity of the people, but a terrifying gloom appears in the descriptions of nature, especially at the conclusions of both works, where nature appears to alienate itself in an orgy of destruction.

The force of water is a motive which both writers use again and again. In *Shadows of Forgotten Ancestors* the dull roar of the Cheremosh River at the very beginning of the novel is used as a leitmotif whenever the protagonist encounters the river until Marichka is carried away by it. The river is never friendly; it turns red from the blood of the feuding families: "down in the valley shimmered ominously the winding Cheremosh with its grey beard, and evil green fire flared up from under the rocks."[1] Marichka's death in the river caused her metamorphosis into a forest elf, which in turn became the direct cause of Ivan's ruin. In *Dorohoiu tsinoiu* (Dearly Bought, 1901) it is again the river which brings destruction. Solomiia fights in vain against the dark waves; the river has already extended its tentacles in the form of reeds, and when she finally tries to save herself by swimming, the river will not release her. The water is here depicted as an obstacle, the border between oppression and freedom, as a black abyss which prevents man's happiness. In *Na kameni* (On the Rock, 1902) the water is also described as an evil force. "For Fatima the sea is the living and constant enemy."[2] Kotsiubyns'kyi's description of the sea in this *Novelle* can be compared with the development of anger in man; slowly the anger develops, intensifies, and then culminates: "The blue sea was excited and foam boiled at the shore... The sea more and more lost its self-control... The grey sea started raving in fury."[3]

Like Kotsiubyns'kyi, Storm also treats water as a natural force which is hostile to mankind. Hauke Haien's self-realization is closely associated with the domination of the sea.[4] By erecting his dike he intends to arrest the destructive forces of the ocean forever[5] but he fails. The sullen animosity of the villagers, their irrational reactions to the work of the dikereeve, are simply another expression of the destructive inroads of elementary forces into rational planning. Like Kotsiubyns'kyi, Storm never shows water as a positive element. Never is it shown as a trade route, as a liveable area, or as a fountain of life. Even fishing is mentioned only in connection with the death of the fisherman.[6]

The symbol of water also appears in Storm's *Novelle Aquis submersus* (1876). Since the protagonist is not engaged in an active struggle, the water is not characterized by the chaotic power it displays toward Hauke Haien. The water's proximity is time and again a parallel to the limited conception of the fate of the lovers, the fleeting quality of love, of fame and beauty. The silvery surface of the sea can be seen from the priest's paddock, but its shimmer is a delusion. The death of the child in the water hole emphasizes the animosity of the element. The impression of fear, especially of the sinister, is also obtained by Storm in *Immensee* by the symbolic use of water. In the episode of the water lilies the water has a sinister, threatening quality, especially when the stems of the water lilies below the dark surface of the lake reach for the protagonist and try to entrap him as in a net.

The function of the water is, therefore, the same with both authors: symbolically and by action it points out the vulnerability of man in the face of disaster and the uncontrollable. F. Martini comments on this subject: [water] "is the symbol of doom, which, planted in man, invades from the natural and supernatural and destroys, no matter how intensive the effort to repulse it. The destructive, a power out of the sphere of the incomprehensible, cannot be stopped.'"[7] The motive of water most clearly illustrates the idea of the omnipresent reality of a hostile fate.

Storm's representation of the sea in *Schimmelreiter* is paralleled by Kotsiubyns'kyi's use of the Carpathian mountain world in *Shadows of Forgotten Ancestors*. This correlation is especially noticeable in Kotsiubyns'kyi's description of Ivan's hike to the mountain pasture: "The shapes of distant peaks of the chain of mountains emerged one by one, they bent their backs, raised themselves like waves of a blue sea. It appeared as if the waves of this sea had solidified exactly at the moment when the storm had raised them from the depths in order to fling them at the earth, flooding everything."[8] The gigantic mountains rise up, dominating all; they are not hospitable to man: "only the brown bear, terrible enemy of domestic animals, called 'uncle' is up to his tricks there."[9] In the mountains Ivan has his meeting with the devil, and the black depths of an abyss finally claims his tired and lovelorn body: "The black, heavy mountain had opened its fir wings and like a bird flew toward the heavens."[10] The world of the mountains confronts the protagonist in a mysterious, cold, and hostile manner.

The forest appears in various works by both writers; however, in *Shadows of Forgotten Ancestors* the forest plays a far more important role than in any of the other novels and short stories. The forests which cover the mountain slopes alternate between friendliness and destructiveness. Actively and dynamically they reach out toward man — sometimes to protect, sometimes to destroy. Often the forest is described as dense, impenetrable, gloomy. In the scene of the meeting with the devil, the forest impedes Ivan's escape from the evil one; the forest frightens the children Ivan and Marichka while they are playing; it appears hostile when Ivan hikes to the mountain pasture. During the Marichka-elf scene the forest is mysterious and sinister, although less so. It is almost as if the forest wanted to prevent Ivan from following the forest elf, as if it were trying to prevent his death. These forest scenes intensify the general sense of the sinister, demonic, and mysterious in the novel. During the trip through the snow-covered forest of Vasylko in *Ialynka* (The Fir Tree, 1891), Kotsiubyns'kyi again paints a threatening, mysterious forest. Storm's forest scenes are more subtle, yet they also arouse a feeling of the threatening and the mysterious. The strawberry scene in *Immensee* brings a sense of dread and the suggestion of danger, while the feeling of danger during the pursuit of Johannes by the Junker in *Aquis submersus* is intensified by the description of the forest.

Not only the descriptions of inanimate nature but also descriptions of animals become mysterious, especially with Storm but also occasionally with Kotsiubyns'kyi. D.S. Artiss, in an examination of the bird motif in *Schimmelreiter* says: "A closer study of the birds in the story reveals the author's 'grand design', for the birds supply the key to the supernatural element and show that Theodor Storm consciously used the bird motif in *Der Schimmelreiter*."[11] Three uses of the bird motif are noted: "Birds appear in the majority of Storm's *Novellen,* often as an incidental nature coloring, frequently as mood symbols reflecting the emotions of the main characters or situations and more selectively and systematically as sinister motifs."[12] Instances of birds as bad omens are the death of Elisabeth's bird in *Immensee,* the "Buhz" in *Aquis submersus* and the death of the seagull Claus in *Der Schimmelreiter.* Seagulls and crows are of special symbolic significance in Storm's last *Novelle.* The final great storm scene which precedes Hauke's end is introduced by the bird motif: "By his side next to the ground, half flying, half flung by the storm, was a flock of white seagulls, calling scornfully. . . ."[13] D.S. Artiss points out that Storm knew, through K. Mullenhoff's collection, of the belief that the seagulls are the souls of the deceased and he interprets their screaming as warnings to Hauke from the chaos of death: "The world of chaos is about to take revenge on Hauke Haien."[14] Also, the seagull of Trin Jans has a special irrational meaning through its connection with the sinister old woman and through her death, since, according to an old belief, the souls of killed seagulls take revenge on man, mostly by bringing misfortune by means of the sea.[15] The destruction of the dike-reeve also cannot be explained satisfactorily by rational considerations. In Kotsiubyns'kyi's *Novelle On the Rock* seagulls are used in a similarly symbolic way in connection with Fatima's death. "Fatima's soul flew to the native village. . . . The blue coat with the yellow half-moons lost its balance and disappeared among the screeching of the lost seagulls."[16]

The crow is considered the worst omen or even as the personification of death. In *Der Schimmelreiter* the connection of the crow motif to the sinister is achieved in the episode of the sea ghost where Hauke "sees the dark shapes"[17] for the first time and where he hears sounds "like the rustling of wings and shrill screeching."[18] In Kotsiubyns'kyi's *Dearly Bought* birds are depicted on several occasions as messengers of bad luck; first there were "flocks of birds — perhaps they were wild geese — that flew over their heads,"[19] then, when Solomiia was lost, "birds that had been startled by her calls circled about her head, screeching anxiously,"[20] . . . "beat with their wings among the reeds and made noises as before a storm . . . circled like clouds above the marsh and screamed so loudly that they drowned the rustling sound of the reeds."[21] Together with vipers, snakes, wild boars and wolves, the birds brought fright and fear of death; they had the same function as Storm's crows.

Storm gives the horse of the dikereeve a connection with the sinister forces of another world, beginning with the manner in which it was purchased: Hauke bought the horse from an unkempt Slovak, who had all the characteristics of a devil. Hauke only gets the horse when he resolves to build his dike, a task that requires superhuman powers. The figure of the grey horse often appears as a symbol of superhuman power in Germanic mythology, for example, Odin's and Balder's horses. The horse can symbolize good or evil forces. In the eyes of the villagers in *Der Schimmelreiter* the mysterious grey horse is a horse of the devil, an apparition from another world.

Other nature motifs with a symbolic meaning appear intermittently and by their positioning often make the correlation of cause and effect questionable. One can note other symbols in Storm's and Kotsiubyns'kyi's writings which do not have sinister connotations, but point to the irrational workings of fate. Most important are descriptions of weather, especially storms, which influence the action, especially in Kotsiubyns'kyi's *Shadows of Forgotten Ancestors* and *Lialechka* (Little Doll, 1901) and in Storm's *Der Schimmelreiter*.

Kotsiubyns'kyi and Storm both point in many different ways

to their tragic conception of fate. They use motifs from myths and the superstitions of their homelands; they personify the mysterious in apparitions of spooks, and they suggest the influence of irrational forces on human action by forebodings and visions understood as parapsychological phenomena. Examples are the symbolic use of color in Kotsiubyns'kyi's *Vin ide* (He Comes, 1906) and Storm's *Immensee;* the appearance of Chyma in *Shadows of Forgotten Ancestors* and Trin Jans in *Der Schimmelreiter;* and the gypsy episodes in *Dearly Bought* and *Immensee.* The mysterious and irrational in the works of Kotsiubyns'kyi and Storm must, therefore, be viewed in a broader connection, as is evident also from other factors. The sinister is only one of a number of ways of indicating the world view of these writers, who believe, paradoxically, in determination.

This contradiction can be discerned in the motivations for action in their stories and *Novellen.* In many cases two explanations for events are suggested. On the one hand, an attempt is made to picture the action as resulting from cause and effect; the event seems determined by circumstances, mere accident, or the apparently inexplicable psychological peculiarities of the characters; the events are placed in a realistic setting and can be understood by factors deriving from the landscape, kinship, or history. On the other hand, this rational view is negated, and often in places where a rational explanation would have been possible. The realism of the action thus becomes highly questionable.

Kotsiubyns'kyi's and Storm's attitude toward such phenomena as superstition, spooks, and apparitions brings up the question whether their repeated appearance in the *Novellen* is to be considered as *fait divers* or whether it is an indication of a larger framework. Kotsiubyns'kyi's intensive study of and occupation with superstition, folklore, and ghost stories point to an interest in occurrences which exceed the span of human senses and intellect. His visits to the funeral ceremonies of the Huzuls and to the sorcerer confirm this interest. This intensive occupation with the irrational was not mere preparation for the Huzul novel, but rather a manifestation of Kotsiubyns'kyi's own ambivalent, searching view of life. M.S. Hrytsiuta comments in an article about *Shadows of Forgotten Ancestors:* "It appears as if Kotsiubyns'kyi was fleeing from the world of reality into the world of fancy."[22] K.F. Boll reports in his analysis *Spuk, Ahnungen und Gesichte bei Theodor Storm* that Storm's library was supposed to have contained many ghost stories and that the author had an extraordinary interest in inexplicable events. In the spring of 1869 he even took a trip to Austria in order to see an apparition with his own eyes at the ancestral castle of the poet von der Traun. Storm's attitude regarding supernatural events is expressed in his own words in a letter to G. Keller: "I view these things in individual instances with doubts or even disbelief; however, in a general sense I submit to them; it is not that I believe the un- or supernatural, but that the natural which does not fall within daily experience has not been recognized yet."[23]

A consideration of the function of the mysterious and irrational in the dualistic works of Kotsiubyns'kyi and Storm brings to the surface another problem: the question of the genesis of their works and of realism. Every work of art can be viewed as a tangible evidence of the philosophy of its creator, even though the artist or writer is unaware of this in most cases. The world pictured in the work of art coincides in its structural elements with the theory of life of the writer. This view of life, in turn, is the result of certain relationships with the social and economic circumstances of the times. The structural relationship of the works of the two writers to nonliterary structures must at least be touched on. The mysterious and irrational must be seen in relationship to the mentalities of the writers and their historical reality. An examination of the world view of the two writers in regard to their attitudes toward God, love, immortality, the empirical world, and fate reveals a certain dualism in both writers. Their view of God — to the small extent to which it can be discerned — is associated with fear and horror; the value of love with loneliness; the idea of immortality with void; the surrender to the empirical world with superstition and the idea of a deterministic fate.

The attitudes of the writers toward questions of faith must be considered the result of the internal struggles of the nineteenth century when most people arrived at a kind of compromise. Storm and Kotsiubyns'kyi rejected faith and transcendence. F. Prykhod'ko specifies the date of Kotsiubyns'kyi's alienation: "since his thirteenth year [he] was an atheist and since his fourteenth year, a socialist."[24] Storm writes about his rejection of faith to Keller: "[I] cannot understand how intellectually trained men can attribute the creation of this cruel world to an all-loving and merciful God."[25] Nevertheless, Christian elements are discernible in Kotsiubyns'kyi and Storm. They adhered in their lives to a moral code based on Christian principles, and both occupied themselves with the problem of death, to which they never found a solution. This agonizing riddle is minimalized in many of their works by a certain depreciation of life. Depictions of suicide, political murder, and pogroms are often used by Kotsiubyns'kyi as a way of lowering the value of mortal life. Death is often linked with tragic love. Oksana in *Concubinage,* Solomiia in *Dearly Bought,* Fatima and Ali in *On the Rock,* as well as Ivan and Marichka in *Shadows of Forgotten Ancestors* find a solution to their problems of love in death. This frequent association points to a centripetal position of death and love in the author's view of life. Kotsiubyns'kyi's treatment of death is discussed from a Soviet point of view by F. Prykhod'ko, who speculates thus: "The theme of death came from the West. Ever more frequently plots appear in which the action is dictated by instinct. Kotsiubyns'kyi avoided this decadent filth, this subconscious idea in which instinct dominates over intellect . . . yet the subject also appears in his works. . . . Solomiia died as a hero. Fatima and Ali left this world romantically. . . . Kotsiubyns'kyi loves his protagonists but he lets them die anyway. . . . Kotsiubyns'kyi carries on a controversy with the writers who support the reactionary philosophy of Nietzsche and Schopenhauer. He decides questions about life and death by his own philosophical plan . . . ."[26] "For the decadents death was the pessimistic eruption of emotion, but for the realist Kotsiubyns'kyi death gives the author the opportunity to treat the theme of life and death philosophically and optimistically."[27] Prykhod'ko's remarks regarding this subject are obscure. Where is the optimism which drives Ivan into the arms of death? Not optimism, but the stark fear of life is described here. Fear is the emotion which Kotsiubyns'kyi treats with special partiality, fear as a reaction to death and transitoriness, and it is intensified by the absence of a Christian belief in immortality. Kotsiubyns'kyi's striking descriptions of this emotion give rise to the conjecture that his understanding of this fear derives not only from his psychological studies but also from his own experience.

Storm's attempts to solve the problem of death lead him on analogous paths. In *Der Schimmelreiter* he shows not only the irrationality of fate; Hauke Haien's death also has the ingredients of a sacrifice. "Guilt weighed so heavily on the dikereeve, that he believed he should offer his life to God as atonement."[28] At the same time, this death is action projected into emptiness since there is no certainty that there is a God who will accept this sacrifice. Storm also depreciates his own trust in the existence of God by invoking fear and horror. In romantic writing horror is given a broader framework, and ghosts are used to discover mysterious ties between this and another world, but Storm uses horror in different way. With him fear tears away the everyday events which obscure man's knowledge of his true situation and his intrinsic loneliness. Fear does not open new possibilities for existence: "If we really ponder, [we realize] that the human creature, each as an individual, lives in terrible loneliness; a lost speck in an unmeasured and incomprehensible fate. We tend to forget this, but once in a while, when faced with the incomprehensible and frightening, we suddenly are overcome by a feeling of it and that, I thought, would be what we usually call horror."[29] Fear, the companion of horror, is closely tied to a lack of a metaphysical faith. Storm sees love as related to this fear: "Love is nothing else but mortal man's fear of loneliness."[30] Storm's rejection of a belief in immortality leads him to couple love with horror and the fear of the transitoriness of all existence.

In spite of their personal rejection of faith in immortality, Kotsiubyns'kyi and Storm retain traditional attitudes toward death. This is evident in their view that respect is owed to the forefathers, as vividly described in Kotsiubyns'kyi's *Shadows of Forgotten Ancestors*. The preservation of traditions, customs, and the moral code of the ancestors is considered extremely important. Storm writes: "The dead also leave a glow on this earth and the descendants should not forget that they are illuminated by this light, so they will keep hands and face unsullied."[31]

Kotsiubyns'kyi's and Storm's conception of fate itself is dualistic. Worldliness, *joi de vivre,* and human plans are again and again destroyed by the predestination of man, which is manifested as heredity, environment, character, or the destructive passage of time. The search for permanence and happiness is overshadowed by the omnipresence of fear and death.

This ambivalence toward major questions of philosophy in both writers results from the broken spirit of life. Their longing for beauty and harmony and their depreciation of these aspirations through depictions of fate and transitoriness were expressions of their social situation. Storm was a representative of the middle class and tried to preserve traditional social relationships, but Kotsiubyns'kyi had gone one step farther toward the age of the great social conflict in Eastern Europe, and he tried to harmonize traditions and customs with the new ideology.

Rather than remaining content with a modest piece of reality, Kotsiubyns'kyi and Storm increasingly attempted in their search for harmony to include the tragic aspects of life. In elucidating their progressively more deterministic philosophy, they used the irrational as a power which exemplifies the paradox of the world and man's abandonment to a world without salvation. The irrational appears in their works not only in the symbolic use of nature and magic — their protagonists themselves are driven by demonic forces. Man is not to be viewed as an autonomous being who can freely forge his own character. It is clear that the mysterious and irrational in the works of Kotsiubyns'kyi and Storm are an expression of their personal philosophy and based on the conflicts in existence which they themselves had experienced.

Elgin, Illinois

NOTES

1. Mychajlo Kozjubyns'kyj, *Schatten vergessener Ahnen,* tr. Anna-Halja Horbatsch (Gottingen, 1966), p. 26; subsequently cited as *Schatten.*
2. F.W. Pustova, "Peisazh u tvorakh M. Kotsiubyns'koho," *Vinok Mykhailu Kotsiubyns'komu* (Kiev, 1967), pp. 156-57.
3. Mykhailo Kotsiubyns'kyi, *Tvory* (6 vols.; Kiev, 1961-62), vol. 2, pp. 118-19; subsequently cited as *Tvory.*
4. The destructive character of the element is clearly indicated during Hauke Haien's first two encounters with the hostile sea, and is intensified as the *Novelle* progresses; see Theodor Storm: *Der Schimmelreiter* (Stuttgart: Reclams Universal-Bibliothek, 1969), pp. 12-13; subsequently cited as *Schimmelreiter.*
5. "The new dike shall stand in spite of these (tidal waves) for hundreds and hundreds of years; it will not be broken through . . . ." *Schimmelreiter,* p. 89.
6. *Schimmelreiter,* pp. 21, 19.
7. F. Martini, *Deutsche Dichter im bürgerlichen Realismus, 1848-1898* (Stuttgart, 1962), p. 664; also D.S. Artiss, "Bird Motif and Myth in Thedor Storm's *Schimmelreiter," Seminar: A Journal of German Studies,* 1968, no. 4, p. 5: "The sea in the *Schimmelreiter* is thus an archetypal image symbolizing the infinite Unknown, huge in dimension and fraught with danger for man's puny world. . . . The sea represents the irrational world of chaos in opposition to Hauke Haien, the 'Aufklarer'."
8. *Schatten,* p. 30.
9. *Schatten,* p. 29.
10. *Schatten,* p. 97.
11. D.S. Artiss, p. 1.
12. D.S. Artiss, p. 3.
13. *Schimmelreiter,* p. 136.
14. D.S. Artiss, p. 6.
15. D.S. Artiss, p. 7.
16. *Tvory,* vol. 2, p. 129.

17. *Schimmelreiter,* p. 15.
18. *Schimmelreiter,* p. 16.
19. *Tvory,* vol. 2, p. 86.
20. *Tvory,* vol. 2, p. 89.
21. *Tvory,* vol. 2, p. 90.
22. M.S. Hrytsiuta, "Folklorna osnova povisti M. Kotsiubyns'koho 'Tini zabutykh predkiv'," *Radians'ke literaturoznavstvo,* 1958, no. 1, p. 59.
23. P. Goldammer, "Zu einigen neueren Publikationen über Theodor Storm," *Weimarer Beiträge,* 1958, no. 4, p. 566.
24. F. Prykhod'ko, *Kotsiubyns'kyi-Novelist* (Kharkov, 1965), p. 3.
25. C. Coler, "Theodor Storm und das Christentum," *Berliner Hefte für geistiges Leben,* 1949, no. 4, p. 363.
26. F. Prykhod'ko, p. 84.
27. Ibid., p. 264.
28. W. Silz, "Theodor Storm's Schimmelreiter," *PMLA,* vol. 61 (1946), p. 767.
29. Quoted from the *Novelle Am Kamin.* See T. Storm, *Werke* (8 vols.; Leipzig: Insel-Verlag, 1923), vol. 2, p. 163.
30. Quoted from T. Storm, "Im Schloss," by C. Coler, "Theodor Storm und das Christentum," p. 369.
31. Theodor Storm, *Sämtliche Werke,* ed. A. Köster (8 vols.; Leipzig, 1919–1929), vol. 2, p. 16.

THE CONTEMPORARY CZECH HISTORICAL NOVEL AND ITS POLITICAL INSPIRATION

WALTER SCHAMSCHULA

Epical art claims to present either real or fictitious events of the past. Consequently, the past tense is the ordinary tense of the art of narrative. Yet the topic of a narrative is not always a matter of the past in a logical sense. A sociocritical novel narrated in the past tense may deal with problems which are still alive in a given society. A utopian novel, as a rule, will be presented in the grammatical past tense as well, but it may try to evoke a vision of the future. Epical fiction becomes definitely a reflection of past events only when it is anchored in history, i.e. when it is unmistakably located in time and space.[1]

The time orientation of a novel which we call logical, be it past, present or future, is subject to literary concepts, fashions, and cultural preferences which, in their way, are dependent on the evolutionary context. There are periods in the history of literature when a preference for the past is nearly universal. In Pushkin's Russia, for example, a historical orientation was essential to the success of a novel.[2] In the forties of the nineteenth century, a preference for the past was suddenly replaced by an orientation towards the present. After World Wars I and II, there were a considerable number of utopian novels which, on the basis of past experiences, tried to develop a vision of a future society, positive or negative.

Historical novels may be frequent at certain periods and rare or totally absent at others. The reasons for such an irregular occurrence are in part aesthetical, owing to an evolution in the art of narrative, and in part social, reflecting certain structures of a given society.

The historical novel as a mirror of certain expectations in the public or as a carrier of a message to the reader may have a variety of social functions: 1) Most frequently it is a call for national unity in periods of distress. 2) Often the author immortalizes the glorious deeds of the ancestors by bringing them to the attention of his readers. 3) The author may use the historical novel as an escape into the past to express opinions which he would not be allowed to express directly. 4) Finally, the historical material may be presented in an intentionally distorted way in order to add a new dimension to history and to specify the author's views ("apocryphal tale").[3]

Whatever message the author may want to convey — patriotic, enlightened, social, moral, religious — he has at his disposal a repertory of devices which the reader can understand and interpret. The ensemble of these devices reflects the novelist's ideology. A first indicator of his world view is his choice of subjects. It is instructive to analyze the historical periods and landscapes treated by certain writers. Alois Jirásek, for example, in his entire voluminous work deals almost exclusively[4] with subjects from Czech history. Non-Czech subjects are rare in Czech historical prose.[5] It is fair to say that in spite of numerous political changes the Czech historical novel has been and continues to be nationalistically oriented.

Also the choice of a certain period of national or international history may be indicative of the author's preferences and political views. To a Czech novelist, the choice of the Hussite period is often like a confession of faith: it may entail a defense of the religious doctrines of the Hussites, a glorification of the most successful warriors in Czech history, or an interpretation of the movement as a social revolution. The Hussite period is the most intensively treated subject of Czech historical prose, from Tyl to Jirásek, Kratochvíl, and Kaplický.

Another indicator of an author's views is the way he presents his heroes. A close-up view of a person's or a nation's life in a novel creates sympathy by participation. When we share the most intimate sensations and experiences of the hero we identify with his personality. The fact that the hero speaks our language or shares our cultural and national background is an additional factor in this process of forming a solidarity. In nationalistically oriented historical novels, as a rule, representatives of a foreign and hostile nation are presented superficially, sketchily, and not closely enough to let us become sympathetic.

As time orientation is a reflection of the cultural and historical situation of a given society, a change in the general atmosphere may cause a sudden shift from one such preference to another. The most dramatic shift of this type took place in the years of the "Protectorate" (1939–1945). Writers who usually wrote about the present, such as Vladislav Vančura, František Křelina, František Kubka, Václav Kaplický, and Miloš Kratochvíl, became past oreinted. Vančura, a prose writer and dramatist of the interwar period who was concerned with the ideals of socialism, started writing a sequence of prose works on national history in a chronicle-like manner: *Obrazy z dějin národa českého* (Pictures from a History of the Czech Nation, 1939, 1940, 1948). While he, a member of the illegal Communist Central Committee, became a victim of the Heydrich affair on June 1, 1942, the other writers survived the war and became historical novelists par excellence. Their turn to national history, which had been a search for the national values at a time of utmost humiliation, became a lasting preference in spite of a temporary return of independence between 1945 and 1948.

Thus the years of the Protectorate are the birthdate of a series of historical novelists whose major political message is that of patriotism. There are, however, certain varieties of world view which should not be overlooked.

František Křelina (born 1903), for instance, was known as a representative of Christian ruralism, a philosophy which connected the Rousseauan concept of the purity of life in nature with

Christianity, and advocated a return to the native soil. He turned to historical fiction under the influence of the year 1939 and published his historical novel *Dcera Královská, blahoslavená Anežka česká* (The King's Daughter, Blessed Agnes of Bohemia) at first in 1941, then in a changed version in 1946 and 1969. This book on the daughter of King Přemysl I, blessed Agnes who died in 1228, carries several messages. In the first place it glorifies a saintly person who, like St. Alexius, preferred a life in chastity to matrimony and all the splendors of a queen, and who did many good works for the poor and sick. In the second place the book conveys the message of patriotism. The Přemyslides are depicted as morally and physically superior to their German contemporaries.[6] In its first version the book also contained a secret code to which the author refers in the epilogue of the 1969 version. Some of these aspects have been eliminated in the last edition. Originally there was a passage in which the author hinted at rumors that after the student revolts of 1939 there were plans to vaccinate Czech children to death. When the danger he was referring to did not materialize the author withdrew the passage from the book.[7] This instance documents a highly politicized use of historical material and an attempt constantly to align its message with the needs of the day. The novel has many good qualities. It is written in a balladic style similar to Vančura's prose. The characters are described as dynamic and strong-willed. The major goal in the 1969 text, however, seems to be the promotion of Christian principles. It is obvious that the book could only be published at certain moments of recent Czech history, that is, prior to 1948 and at the last stage of the "Prague Spring."

Patriotism, thus, has been the major inspiration of the new historical novelists. Yet this type of national propaganda was subjected to reinterpretation at the beginning of 1948, and the results of this revision are still evident.

In the work of Miloš Václav Kratochvíl (born 1904) we observe two periods of historical fiction: a) first, psychologically developed novels centered around single heroes, and b) after 1950, the adoption of the principles of dialectical materialism, an emphasis on the role of the popular masses and extensive reasoning about the mechanism of history. These dry elaborations on the social history of the country may become quite prevalent; one of Kratochvíl's most recent biographical novels, *Život Jana Amose* (The Life of Jan Amos [i.e. Comenius], 1975) became a hybrid form of *biographie romancée* and scholarly monograph. Here the author even abstains from the close-up perspective which is the essence of effective narrative prose. Instead of presenting Komenský as a living person with all his emotions, he offers a scholarly analysis of his intellectual growth and stays outside his psyche.

Kratochvíl's subjects are taken exclusively from two periods of Czech history: Hussitism and the Thirty Years' War. Before 1950 he concentrates on the intimate life and the psychological experiences of a hero like King Wenceslaus IV (*Král obléká halenu,* The King Puts on the Frock, 1945). But he becomes overly didactic in his Hussite trilogy, of which only two parts have materialized: *Pochodeň* (The Torch, 1950), and *Mistr Jan* (Master John, 1951). The explanations of history as a class struggle are sometimes presented as in a school handbook. This is the case in *Mistr Jan:* "But besides the townsfolk, the craftsmen, merchants and buyers, there are today and always are . . . those who cannot buy anything . . . because they can offer only their hands, which no one wants, and beyond that they meet only misery and hunger: the laborers, hired hands, and young journeymen without work. All those who may earn a needed trifle two or three times a week, too little for a living and too much for dying . . ."[8] In spite of this turn to historical didacticism Kratochvíl continues to display his mastery of language and description.

Unlike Kratochvíl, Václav Kaplický (born 1895) almost never ceases to fascinate his readers even during the fifties when he adopts the official doctrine of history. Kaplický, too, began writing historical novels during the Nazi occupation. The fact that during the "Protectorate" there was no school instruction in Czech history inspired him to write his first Hussite novel in 1944: *Kraj kalicha* (The Land of the Chalice) which was published in 1945.[9] The tendency of the book is patriotic, and the specifically Hussite messianic claim of the Czechs to be God's own nation has survived in a somewhat secularized form; Kaplický states in the epilogue: "From Huss's stake and from Žižka's Tábor there is a straight path to our days. It is the longing of the Czech people for truth, freedom, and justice. Through all these five hundred years the conflict has remained basically the same; only the weapons and the forms of that struggle have changed."[10] Kaplický's shift from nationalistically inspired historical prose to the kind of narrative which reflects dialectical materialism is evident, as has been bluntly indicated by his biographer Jaromíra Nejedlá with reference to the second edition of *Kraj kalicha:* "When Kaplický in 1955 published his *Kraj kalicha* for the second time, the novel already had the shape of a mature work of art, purified in terms of language, style and thought (myšlenkově)."[11]

Kaplický's works in the fifties show an obsession with the idea of the popular masses as the carriers of history, as is the case in *Čtveráci* (The Rogues, set in the Thirty Years' War, 1952), *Smršť* (The Cyclone, end of the eighteenth century, 1955), *Železná koruna* (The Iron Crown, reign of Emperor Leopold I, 1954), and *Rekruti* (The Recruits, period of the early French Revolution in Bohemia, 1956).

There are indications that Kaplický joined the general trend of the sixties towards a humanization and dedoctrinization of literature. One good example is *Kladivo na čarodějnice* (A Hammer against Witches, 1963), a novel on the witch hunt of the seventeenth century. On the surface the book is fully in line with the official doctrine: it attacks "superstition" and abuses of ecclesiastical power, yet it is not totally antireligious. There are victims of the witch hunt even within the church hierarchy, for example, the dean Lautner who ends up at the stake together with many alleged witches. The chief prosecutor Boblig, though Christian by name, is a mere "apparatchik" and considers his only source of wisdom the infamous guideline for the persecution of witches, *Malleus maleficarum,* rather than the Bible.[12] In the Czech cultural context, where coded messages are very common or even the only possible messages to the reader, the novel could be interpreted as directed against absolute power, the monopoly of doctrine, and the witch hunt of the seventeenth century could serve as an allegory of the "cult of personality."[13]

In 1969, in his novel *Táborská republika* (The Tábor Republic), Kaplický seems to return to the concept of the people as the carrier of history: "not the romantic heroes...but the people are the carriers of history."[14] Interestingly enough, Kaplický also returns to the Hussite period, with its inexhaustible repertory of subjects with "the people acting." In the seventies he still prefers to treat subjects where the basic conflict is created by the confrontation of the masses of common people and their superiors. This is the case in novels on revolts against the authorities, such as in *Škůdce zemský Jiří Kopidlanský* (The Country Pest Jiří Kopidlanský, 1976). Kopidlanský, a Robin Hood of an outcast, fights injustice in the early sixteenth century by redistributing goods — taking from the rich and giving to the poor. Kopidlanský becomes, however, a romantic hero like Nikola Šuhaj or Oleksa Dobvuš in Ivan Olbracht's *Nikola Šuhaj Loupežník,* and in spite of the fact that he is presented in a rather objective, narrative way, without much psychology, and without interior monologues. It seems that in the seventies we see only an incomplete return to the principles of the fifties. This is the case in *Kdo s koho* (Who Will Overcome, 1979) where the author continues to focus on the rebels of the time of King Vladislav — Zdeněk Malovec z Chýnova and Oldřich Janovský z Janovic. The political message the reader gets from the novel is that at this stage of feudalism certain members of the gentry try to oppose the central power, take refuge in absolute lawlessness and disorder, cause the country to be exposed to foreign invasions and finally to succumb to such an invasion, namely in 1620 in the Battle of White Mountain. Thus the novel may be understood as a call for unity — but in view of which threat? Should we read it as a parable on the events of 1968, or 1938? Or is it rather one of the commonplace calls for watchfulness in view of an alleged NATO Alliance threat? It is hard to decode the message, and it seems that certain vestiges of slogans of the past have survived in the historical novel of the seventies.

One of the most fascinating authors of historical prose in postwar Czechoslovakia was František Kubka (1894 – 1969), who died before any consequences of the 1968 invasion could affect him. He started his career as a writer and a historian of literature before World War I. After a period of silence caused by Julius Fučík's severe attack on his *St. Wenceslaus Play* (Hra svatováclavská, 1929) his interest in history and historical prose was revived by the war. Especially his cycle of novellas around Charles IV, *Karlštejnské vigilie*[15] (The Karlstein Vigils, 1944) are, both in form (neoclassical) and content, part of Kubka's patriotic message. This participation in contemporary political life by way of historical fiction remained Kubka's trademark also in the following period. Kubka's Paleček novels: *Palečkův úsměv* (Paleček's Smile, 1946) and *Palečkův pláč* (Paleček's Tears, 1948) are also neoclassical. The first volume was written during the war, which is reflected clearly in the book. The trauma of the Munich agreement affected this set of novels and influenced deeply the image of its hero. At first, Kubka wanted to create a Czech Eulenspiegel, a public clown whom he intended to accompany King George of Poděbrady. Under the influence of the occupation, however, the author changed Paleček into a kind of St. Francis of Assisi who has the supernatural gift of talking with the birds. Moreover, Paleček is like a picaresque hero who passes through history like a sacred fool and reflects history in his undisturbed mind. His servant, Matěj Bradýř, a kind of Sancho Panza, is a Taborite. To Kubka, the Hussite tradition is identical with good patriotic traditions. He seems to refer to Dalimil when he compares Venice to Prague: "My city. . .is like the bird Phoenix rejuvenated by fire. My city grumbles, my city swings in its interior brawl, my city is torn apart by the struggles of her sons. But from the struggles, the brawls, from the faith and love of these sons my city is growing into glory. My city sings the glorious song of stone and power, of courage and faith. And this is the song of the warriors of God."[16] This, again, is the Messianic concept of the Hussite tradition. More specific is Kubka's description of the social and

Contemporary Czech Historical Novel

national situation in Tábor during the reign of George of Poděbrady: "We have enough foreigners here among us. All of them are faithful brethren and oftimes more expert at the words of Master John than we Czechs ourselves. There are Englishmen, old fellows, from among the disciples of Master English (i.e. Peter Payne), there are Hungarians, only the Germans do not stay. They, too, became attracted by the chalice, but then they left for their home, or at least to the neighborhood, to the domains of the Rosenbergs. Our life is not their life, and we and they are better off when we are apart."[17] This was published in the year of the forced expatriation of the German minority from Czechoslovakia, which it seems to justify. This chapter of Czech history, by the way, is taboo in Czech historical literature and mentioned only marginally.

Related to the Paleček theme are two other historical novels which Kubka created around the figure of Ječmínek, *Říkali mu Ječmínek* (They Called Him Ječmínek, 1957) and *Ječmínkův návrat* (Ječmínek's Return, 1958). Ječmínek is the page of the Bohemian queen, wife of the "Winter-king" Frederick who was defeated at the Battle of White Mountain. More than a page, Ječmínek is the queen's lover and the father of her son. The love affair and Ječmínek's adventures take place during the fundamental changes caused by the Thirty Years' War and are designed to serve as a message to the contemporaries. In an interview with *Lidová demokracie,* the author himself explained his didactical intentions: "By its location in time the novel on Ječmínek has become a novel on Munich with a time shift of three hundred years. I think that these centuries do not deprive the novel of its topicality, because the essence of both tragedies — of White Mountain and of Munich — is the same.[18]

Summing up our previous findings we may say that in historical fiction the late forties reflect patriotic tendencies as a result of the experiences of war and occupation, the fifties emphasize the role of the people as the moving force of history within the concept of history as class struggle. The sixties are characterized by a certain relaxation of this concept and a return to the personality of the hero and to narrative as art. The seventies, from what we have seen in Kaplický's or Kratochvíl's works, do not reverse the situation totally, but seem to effect a compromise between the tendencies of the fifties and of the sixties. The values presented are the traditional ones without a conclusive connection with the present situation. It may be too early for a general statement of this kind, yet one of the most recent historical novels, Jiří Brabenec' *Řeka osudu* (River of Destiny, 1979), seems to support it. This novel, incidentally one of the first postwar historical novels to show some formal inventiveness, and the first on the life of the Czech Renaissance chronicler Hájek z Libočan, addresses many of the topics mentioned above. There is patriotism in connection with the religious movements of the Hussite tradition: Calixtines and Bohemian Brethren are generally the "good guys" as opposed to the Lutherans. There is also criticism of Rome and the Catholic church and of the priesthood in general. The most respectable character of the novel is Jan Hodějovský z Hodějova who is a humanist and a skeptic. There are also references to the social tensions of the time, praise of the peasants and lower classes, without, however, making it the central issue of the book, references to the poor condition of the Jews in sixteenth-century Bohemia, etc. There are aspects one could encounter elsewhere in Czech historical novels of the postwar period, but none of them appears to be dominating. Besides, there are many details of history which could be interpreted as coded messages. The person of Emperor Ferdinand who, after receiving the mandate, starts ruling despotically, reminds us of Stalin.[19] The upheaval in Prague where the party of Pašek defeats Hlavsa's party could be a paradigm of the February 1948 overthrow of the democratic government.[20] There is no proof that the author really meant to associate these events: every reader, according to his personal experiences, may interpret them individually.

Řeka osudu thus appears to be a historical novel with many political aspects, all of which are presented without zeal, almost like commonplaces and excuses. The book seems to concentrate on the narrative and on the popular presentation of the historical facts which are accompanied by illustrations and numerous reproductions of pictures contemporary to the events. This is one more evidence of a certain retreat from topicality in the historical novel of the seventies. Other examples are the series of historical novels dealing with nonpolitical issues, such as Kaplický's *Život alchimistův* (The Life of the Alchemists, 1980), Kratochvíl's *Láský královské* (The Kingly Loves [on the Přemyslide queens], 1980), or the rise of a historical detective novel: Oldřich Daněk's *Vražda v Olomouci* (Murder in Olomouc, 1972).

In Czech literature of the postwar period the historical novel is not the key genre, popular as it may be. Independent as it is because of its specific material, it still shares many of the developments of contemporary Czech literature. Its inherent qualities and structures may, however, be fully appreciated later when the preference for the past will have come to an end and the historical novel after World War II will be more seizable as an entity than it is today.

University of California at Berkeley

NOTES

1. At this point I am not trying to define historical prose or the historical novel, yet I want to express my agreement with the generally accepted notion that a novel becomes historical when its topic is removed from the author far enough to make it a subject of scholarly inquiries rather than a reflection of his personal experiences. For detailed discussions of a variety of devices in historical narrative see my study "On the Types of Historical Narrative in Slavic Literatures," *PTL, A Journal for Descriptive Poetics and Theory of Literature,* 1979, no. 4, pp. 133–43.

2. See W. Schamschula, "Der russische historische Roman vom Klassizismus bis zur Romantik," *Frankfurter Abhandlungen zur Slavistik,* vol. 3 (1961), p. 143.

3. See W.E. Harkins, *Karel Čapek* (New York, 1962), pp. 159–61; and Schamschula, "On the Types of Historical Narrative," p. 138 f.

4. The only novel in Jirásek's oeuvre dealing with a non-Czech subject, "Ráj světa" (The Paradise of the World, in *Lumír,* 1880), still shows

some connection with novels on Czech subjects, especially *Na dvoře vévodském,* and tries to develop the idea of Czech nationalsim by showing the negative aspects of the society of diplomats at the Congress of Vienna.

4. The only prominent historical novel on a non-Czech subject after the war is Josef Toman's *Po nás potopa* (1967) with a topical use of Roman history.

6. Cf. the tournament between Vratislav and Frederick, the description of which seems to be inspired by the Old Czech story of *Štilfríd* (Prague, 1969), p. 104.

7. Ibid., p. 221.

8. *Mistr Jan* (Prague, 1951), p. 12. All texts are translated by the author.

9. See Jaromíra Nejedlá, *Václav Kaplický* (Prague, 1975), p. 100.

10. Ibid., p. 103.

11. Ibid., p. 106.

12. *Kladivo na čarodějnice* (Prague, 1963), p. 58.

13. See Heinrich Kunstmann, *Tschechische Erzählkunst im 20. Jahrhundert* (Cologne and Vienna, 1974), p. 187.

14. Ibid.

15. See W. Schamschula, "Tschechische Dichtung um Karl IV," *Kaiser Karl IV, Staatsmann und Mäzen,* ed. F. Seibt (Munich, 1978), pp. 407 – 10.

16. *Palečkův úsměv* (Prague, 1949), p. 271.

17. Ibid., p. 233.

18. See the cover text of *Říkali mu Ječmínek* (Prague, 1957).

19. *Řeka osudu* (Prague, 1979), p. 332.

20. Ibid., p. 165 f.

HISTORY AS FICTION:
THE NOVELS OF TEODOR PARNICKI

WOJCIECH SKALMOWSKI

The entire oeuvre of Parnicki consists of more than twenty novels in Polish published between 1937 and 1976. With the exception of one book which has been translated into Russian,[1] his novels have not been translated into foreign languages. They belong to the domain of the historical novel, but they are interconnected — often *ex post facto* — and form a heterogenous whole. The aim of this paper is to assess the oeuvre, its form and content, and its place in literature.

Parnicki's biography is an important element of his literary work both indirectly, as a source of creative impulses and directly, as a subject of his later works, and for this reason it must be dealt with here at some length.[2]

His family was of Polish origin, from Wielkopolska, but in the nineteenth century it found itself on the verge of Germanization. August Parnitzki (sic) — the grandfather of Teodor — was a Prussian noncommissioned officer in the war of 1870, but later he settled in Russia and worked as a technician. His son Bronisław — the father — was sent down from Kiev University for political activity and went to Berlin, where he studied engineering. He married his Jewish fiancée from Kiev, Augustyna Piekarska, and their first son Teodor was born in 1908 in Berlin. When he had finished his studies Bronisław Parnicki returned with his family to Russia. After the death of his first wife in 1918 he married a

Russian woman who apparently strongly disliked her stepsons (Teodor had a younger brother). In 1919 Teodor was sent to a preparatory military school in Omsk, which was soon evacuated to Vladivostok. In 1920 Teodor ran away from this school and went to Kharbin in Chinese Manchuria, where he expected to find a friend of his father. He was not met there, but the Polish colony in Kharbin took care of him and sent him to a local Polish high school, from which he graduated in 1927. This was the period of his reintegration into Polish culture (at home he spoke mostly German and Russian). From reading historical novels, especially those of Henryk Sienkiewicz (1846 – 1916), he resolved at the age of fifteen to become a writer of historical fiction.

A brilliant student at the high school, he received a scholarship from the Polish government for further studies in Poland. Arriving there in 1928, a few months after the death of his father whom he had not seen since 1919, Parnicki enrolled in the Jan Kazimierz University in Lwow. There he studied Polish literature under Prof. J. Kleiner, the well-known specialist in Polish romantic poetry, and attended courses in English and Oriental philology. Parnicki never formally finished his studies, partly because he engaged in journalism, literary work, and lecturing (he even gave courses in modern Russian literature at the University). At that time he was already a prolific writer (in 1931 he once wrote a full-length theater play in 14 hours), but his first serious work *Aetius, the Last Roman* appeared only in 1937. This novel won him a scholarship from the Polish Academy of Literature, which allowed him to make a voyage in 1939 through Bulgaria, Turkey, and Greece to Italy, from where he returned to Lwow five days before the outbreak of World War II.

After the occupation of Eastern Poland by the Soviet Union in 1939 Parnicki, sharing the fate of about one and a half million other Polish citizens, was imprisoned and deported to Russia. After the German attack on Russia in 1941 Parnicki was liberated and joined the staff of the Polish Embassy of Sikorski's Government in Exile. In 1943, after Stalin had broken with this government, Parnicki, who served as press attaché, left for Teheran.

From there via Iraq, Syria, and Lebanon he went to Palestine, where he was allowed to settle in a semiofficial capacity so that he could finish his second important novel, *Silver Eagles*. He found his materials in the library of the Hebrew University in Jerusalem. This book was printed in 1944, had an immediate success among Polish readers throughout the world, and is still his most famous novel.

In the same year he was summoned by the Government in Exile to London and sent from there as a cultural attaché to the Polish Embassy in Mexico. After the withdrawal of recognition for the Government in Exile by the Western Allies in 1945 his diplomatic career (together with the steady income) came to an end, but Parnicki remained in Mexico. Thanks to Polish émigré institutions and private aid he continued his literary activity; but as an emigrant in the West he could no longer count on an easy access to readers in Communist Poland. His *Silver Eagles* appeared there in 1949, but in the Stalinist period it became a forbidden book and was withdrawn from circulation. His following book, *The End of the "Concord of Nations,"* written in Mexico, could at first be published only abroad (Paris: Biblioteka "Kultury," 1955).

It was not until 1956, during "the thaw" that he again became printable in Poland. Pax, a pro-Communist organization of the "socially progressive Catholics," which had at its disposal important financial means, initiated his comeback first in spirit, by reissuing his earlier books and printing the new ones, and later in the flesh. After two long visits, in 1963 and 1965, Parnicki returned to Poland permanently in 1967 and since that time has lived and worked in Warsaw.

Because of its sheer size, Parnicki's oeuvre can be described only in a sketchy way. Two different chronologies must be taken into account in order to situate and describe the novels: first the historical epoch in which a given novel is set, and second, the time at which it was written. The universe of Parnicki's oeuvre comprises some two thousand years of history and a territory stretching from Central Asia to America. His literary style has changed with time; generally speaking, the novels have become increasingly obscure, fantastic, and autothematic, and his later works are incomprehensible without a knowledge of the preceding ones. As has been observed by M. Czermińska, "the novels of Parnicki should be read in the chronological order of their appearance, but in order to write about them one has to proceed in the opposite way — one has to start at the end, beginning with the very last novel printed."[3] The historical settings of Parnicki's works can be divided into four periods which will be discussed in the order of real chronology.

As for antiquity, Parnicki is particularly interested in the second century B.C. and the fifth A.D. Two novels deal with the first period. *The End of the "Concord of Nations"* is set in the Bactrian, Greek-dominated kingdom of the Eutidemid dynasty in Central Asia. The title of the book is also the name of a ship on the Amu-Daria — the name itself expresses the political program of the dynasty. An elaborate investigation of this dynasty has the stated aim of establishing the identity of Leptynes, a half-Greek and half-Jew, who has assassinated a Roman envoy in Syria. The same character is also the hero of *Circles on the Sand,* a novel consisting of his memoirs written in a prison in Rome.

The late antique period features the figure of Aetius, a Roman military commander and dictator under the emperor Valentinian III, by whose hand he fell in 454 A.D. In *Aetius, the Last Roman* the hero is described at the top of his career and success (the defense of Rome against the Huns); in *The Death of Aetius* the hidden springs of his assassination are being investigated, and in *The Moon's Face,* Part 2, the Roman scene at the time of Aetius is viewed from Byzantium. A part of *Kill Cleopatra* is also set in this period and forms a continuation of the above mentioned novels, but its Parts 2 and 3 are set in later times.

Set in a time between the two favored periods is the epistolary novel *Word and Flesh.* It consists of letters by two characters living in Alexandria at the beginning of the second century A.D., the Parthian prince Chosroes, held there as a hostage of the Romans, and Marcia, a former mistress of the emperor Commodus, who was murdered in 192. The real identity of the two correspondents is soon brought into question and the reader is left in uncertainty as to whether the texts (Word) really represent their pretended authors (Flesh).

Five novels are set in the medieval period: *The Moon's Face,* Part 3; *Silver Eagles; The New Fable,* vols. 1 and 2; and *Only Beatrice.* The earliest in historical setting is the epilogue of *The Moon's Face,* a tripartite cycle describing an imaginary family clan originated in the third century A.D. by a Chorasmian princess Mitroania, who had been brought to the Roman Empire as a captive and whose descendants later held important political positions throughout the world. Part 3 of this cycle describes a meeting of the clan members which takes place in the ruins of a castle of Chosroes (see *Word and Flesh*) in the Caucasus. The anonymous participants — they wear masks — discuss during one week the necessity of defending Europe against the Arab conquest. The novel suggests that they formed a special detachment in the battle of Poitiers in 732, which was decisive in the victory of the Franks.

The New Fable is a loosely constructed cycle and its separate novels are connected chiefly by means of imaginary, and quite fantastic, genealogical relationships. Its first volume, *The Workers Summoned at Eleven* (an allusion to the recently Christianized nations), is situated in the Poland of Bolesław the Bold (ca. 1040 – 81) and centers around an interminable conversation between the dying abbot Aron (a vaguely historical figure who is the main character in *Silver Eagles*) and Stanisław of Szczepanowo (the historical bishop and martyr, assassinated for political reasons in 1078). Their conversation treats the whole complex of European medieval legends — Aron is allegedly of Irish origin — and it is hinted that their content expresses some secret knowledge, probably about the existence of America. This last motif is developed further in the cycle's second volume, in which Joan of Arc was supposedly deported to the Mexico of the Aztecs.

Silver Eagles deals with the Poland of Bolesław the Brave (ca. 966 – 1025), who was made Patrician of the Roman Empire by

Otto III (the title alludes to the symbol of this dignity) but the events form only a fragment of a vast political game among Rome, Germany, and Byzantium. The reader regards the scene from the point of view of Aron, a protégé of the Pope Silvester II.

Only Beatrice is set in the beginning of the fourteenth century, partly in Poland and partly in Avignon at the court of the Pope John XXII. This novel, regarded as one of Parnicki's masterpieces, illustrates particularly well his method of interweaving history with fantasy and literary allusions. The title refers to a passage from a Polish poem by Jan Lechoń (1899 – 1956), which says:

> There is no earth nor heaven, no limbo nor hell,
> There is only Beatrice . . . . and she doesn't exist either.

These lines, which are used as the novel's motto, synthetize its two main plots, the growth of a heresy (the historical Pope John XXII believed that the Last Things would take shape only after the Last Judgment and for the time being were nonexistent) and the passionate love of the hero, the half-breed Stanisław the Deacon, for princess Rixa Elisabeth, the daughter of the assassinated Polish prince Przemysław II (1257 – 1296) and later queen of Bohemia. The elusiveness of events, including a strong suggestion that the love affair is only an illusion of the hero, and frequent literary allusions to Dante, make this book comparable with Nabokov's *Pale Fire*.

Three novels are set in the early modern period and concern two interconnected themes, the conquest of Mexico by Cortez and Polish-Swedish political relationships in the seventeenth century. *The New Fable,* vol. 3, *Labyrinth,* connects an unsuccessful conspiracy against Cortez in a truly labyrinthine way with events in Poland and Ruthenia 500 years earlier. Several characters of this novel reappear in the next volume of the cycle, *Earthen Jugs* (an allusion to a poem by Leopold Staff, 1878 – 1957), which is set in a castle in Nyköping in Sweden, where several characters are imprisoned for ten years. A complicated intrigue, dealing with a maze of falsified biographies, changes of names and pretended identities, should suggest to the reader that the English playwright

Christopher Marlowe was not actually killed in Deptford in 1593, but had before this date exchanged his "life role" with the (imaginary) Pole Mateusz Boniecki and had an illegitimate son, who later became known as Jan Onufrius Zagłoba. It should be recalled that Zagłoba is a Falstaff-like character of the historical trilogy by Henryk Sienkiewicz. As an additional tour de force Parnicki lets the reader understand that his own family is related to Zagłoba.

A more detailed account of Zagłoba's life before he appeared in Sienkiewicz's books is given by Parnicki in a novel published a year before *Earthen Jugs* and bearing the bizarre title *With the Mighty Ones Strange Too* (a quotation from P. Skarga, 1535 – 1612, the chaplain of Sigismund III Vasa and author of famous sermons). The book is in the form of memoirs by the hero and presents him, in deliberate opposition to Sienkiewicz's picture, as an intellectual, a gifted playwright (the heritage of Marlowe, no doubt!), and an aspiring Jesuit. This last ambition is finally frustrated because, due to his partly Jewish ancestry through his mother, Zagłoba is not accepted by the Jesuit order. He decides to change completely his way of life and turns into the picturesque buffoon of Sienkiewicz.

The first part of the fifth volume of *The New Fable* cycle, *Hatcheries of Marvels,* is a complicated science fiction novel allegedly written in the seventeenth century and describing the Poland of the tenth century; this part has a separate title, *A New Tale about the Lentil Dish, or Fable of Fables*. Part 2, with a still stranger title, *A Charming Lady from the Inscription on a Hat and on a Banner,* tries to establish who might have written Part 1, a "future utopia" describing the twentieth-century world governed by the so-called New Order, a kind of totalitarian communism (this term is not used) based on "general expropriation" and caste-like stratifications of society. A counterfactual "history" built into the novel traces the origin of this system back to the Great Turn in 1636, when a group of sages operating from Bersalem Island (an allusion to Francis Bacon) took power thanks to their invention of wings for humans and submarines. The Christian Church collaborated by developing a suitable form of doctrine, a sell-out to which the "lentil dish" in the title alludes, whereas the last true popes, Jewish by the way, live as refugees in Jerusalem.

The remaining novels of Parnicki are chiefly set in the nineteenth century, insofar as they can be regarded as being set anywhere. The protagonist of *A Different Life of Cleopatra* is Edmund Dantes, the hero of A. Dumas' *Count of Monte Cristo*, and he is preoccupied in Parnicki's novel with deterring someone from writing a fantastic historical novel about Cleopatra based on the assumption that she had survived Antony's fall and made her way to India. Fiction as the subject of fiction is also the technique of *The Muse of Far Voyages* (a quotation from a poem by N.S. Gumilev, 1886–1921) and its continuation *We Stood There Like Two Dreams* (a quotation from an ambiguous line in "Beniowski" by Juliusz Słowacki, 1809–1849). In fact *The Muse* includes two unwritten novels; one describes the imaginary Fourth Kingdom of Poland, which came into being after the — counterfactual — victory of the Poles in their uprising against Russia in 1830; the other describes in a sketchy way the first Slavic state of Samon, who — according to vague historical sources — ruled in the Balkans in the seventh century. The unifying third plot is autobiographical and autothematic. In order to combine all the three plots a "time machine" is introduced. This device unfortunately makes its appearance in a few other novels by Parnicki and the naïveté of this trick contrasts sharply with the elaborateness of his other literary techniques.

Parnicki gradually became unable to write a straightforward historical novel, even in the fantastic convention, and began to use plots of planned books as pretexts for reflections on his work and life. This is the case with *Identity*, which blends depictions of a figure known in Biblical studies as "the second Isaiah" (ca. sixth century, B.C.) with another plot where Parnicki's grandfather August is the central character; it is frequently hinted that the whole "action" takes place in his grandson's mind. The last books hover between diary and essay in the form of Platonic dialogue or, as their author chooses to call them, "dramatic fragments." However great their importance for the interpretation of the oeuvre may be, the pretense that they are still novels is difficult to maintain.

The second important parameter of Parnicki's novels is the time when they were written, because their content, the origin of their characters, and their stylistic techniques changed considerably with time.

Parnicki himself described his work (in *Finger of Menace* and *The Muse*) as a mixture of history, fantasy, autobiography, and metaphysics. This mixture varies with the periods of his creative activity. Only his first two novels, *Aetius* and *Silver Eagles,* can be regarded as historical novels in the traditional sense of describing past events. The third novel, *The End of the "Concord of Nations,"* introduces a fantastic motif, a steamship in the second century B.C., a device which plays a role in the historiosophic parts of the book, and which is a reflection on what would have happened if technical progress had started in antiquity. In later novels the role of fantastic motifs grows steadily. They usually appear in the form of anachronisms and/or fantastic genealogies. Among anachronisms must be counted the assumption that there was secret knowledge of the Copernican system in antiquity and of the existence of America in the Middle Ages. One could speak of a mutual contamination of the fantastic and the metaphysical, because at the bottom of Parnicki's interest in the spiritual cultures of former epochs (only in the first novels are there scanty descriptions of the surroundings) often lies the suggestion that mythologies, creeds, and literary works of the past contain some hidden information about reality, whether coded factual knowledge or transformations of the secret ambitions and plans of humans.

Examples of fantastic genealogies have already been mentioned, and there are many more. In *The New Fable* St. Stanisław of Szczepanowo is pictured as an illegitimate son of Bolesław the Bold and Predslava, the daughter of Vladimir, prince of Kiev (thus he would be a nephew of Boris and Gleb). Similarly, Stanisław the Deacon in *Only Beatrice* reveals himself (in *Kill Cleopatra*) as a distant descendant of Mitroania of *The Moon's Face*. Without much exaggeration it could be said that nearly all the characters of Parnicki's oeuvre are related to each other and very often they have improbable relatives among historical and literary characters throughout the world.

Parnicki's characters may be historical, vaguely historical (his favorites), imaginary, or himself, or personifications of abstract notions. The old method of mixing real and imaginary characters, developed by Dumas and Sienkiewicz, is combined by Parnicki with "romantic irony," that is, the abandonment of realistic conventions. Gradually all kinds of characters might be introduced and finally the barriers of time and space became superfluous. The subject became "the mutual interdependence between the creator of the literary work and his characters" (*Kill Cleopatra*).[4] The last volume of *The New Fable, Finger of Menace* (another quotation from Słowacki), may be regarded as the culmination ot this development and the beginning of a new phase in Parnicki's oeuvre. In this novel a kind of trial of the author is organized by the characters of the cycle, and certain abstract notions (e.g. "Silver — the art of historical writing") make their appearance. Further works continue this new convention: the largely autobiographical *Transformation* even splits the author himself into Tau, Pseudo-Tau and Super-Tau, clearly the Freudian Ego, Superego and Id.

This evolution was facilitated by the substitution of direct speech for indirect speech. Only the three first novels still have an omniscient narrator. After *Word and Flesh,* an epistolary novel, the reader is confronted with the characters only through their utterances. Various forms serve as vehicles: fragments of documents, memoirs, reports, etc.; often they are provided with additional remarks and commentaries by, allegedly, other characters. A favorite technique is the imaginary dialogue, which characters carry on with themselves, and which is given *in extenso*. The novels are frequently staged as an interrogation, trial, or conference and the reader is presented with protocols and notes, full of tedious procedural details. Usually the reader is obliged to guess, because no initial information is provided, who is speaking (characters often bear cryptonyms), and where and when the action is situated.

This deliberate obscurity, originally intended as an imitation of the actual difficulties in discovering historical truth in incomplete sources, was later employed for its own sake and introduced into the oeuvre to make it still more self-sufficient and hermetic. In later novels the characters often discuss the question of who could have written the preceding part of the book.

Parnicki's style contributes its own obscurity. He writes in a peculiar language, syntactically stylized to resemble Latin (perhaps the influence of Sienkiewicz's *Quo vadis*), with interminable sentences abounding in subordinate clauses.[5] A special effect, giving rather the impression of mannerism than archaism, is created by frequent inversions. Highly literary expressions or slang words are used as if they belonged to normal cultivated Polish, and there are intercalations of foreign words and phrases. This last trait may be viewed as a part of a general tendency to use quotations and literary allusions. They are often hidden in the text as additional elements of a puzzle presented to the reader.[6] They have several functions (the Shakespearean allusions in *Earthen Jugs* stress the alleged substitution of Marlowe for Boniecki), but the chief motive for their increasing use is obvious: to extend the universe of discourse in a mental direction. They help to translocate the oeuvre to where it actually always was situated, namely in the consciousness of Parnicki himself.

Parnicki's oeuvre is not a homogenous whole, even if he wanted to make it into one *ex post facto*,[7] but it has certain thematic invariants which can be called "central ideas." His novels usually center around two notions: that of half-breeds (*mieszańcy*) and that of political power.

The favorite characters of Parnicki are of mixed ethnic, cultural, and/or religious origin. Leaving aside the question as to how far Parnicki's fascination with half-breeds stems from his own experience, and it is obvious that he has had difficulties in establishing his national identity, he is interested in them for other psychological and sociological reasons. According to him, half-breeds are all those who "are aware, realize and feel that there is no place for them within the community into which they have been born" (*Earthen Jugs*).[8] This condition makes them suffer but also stimulates them into activity. They are driven, often subconsciously, either to discover through exaggerated efforts some part of their divided identity, or become revolutionaries, at least in spirit. It is the half-breeds who invent utopias and supranational creeds or dream of a "counter-earth," where they would shed their stigma of nonbelonging. They are the driving force of history, at least of the history of ideas, and try to change the rigidly established structures which constitute their surroundings.

These structures are rooted in the political power held by the mighty. Parnicki visualizes power as the possibility of manipulating others and of establishing impassable barriers. It is tacitly assumed, in nearly an Adlerian fashion, that hunger for power is the motivating force of human behavior. The half-breeds themselves are not immune to it — they are only powerless. When their dreams come true, and Parnicki is keenly interested in the materialization of dreams in history, they become oppressors themselves (cf. the New Order in *Hatcheries of Marvels*), or they get duped by still cleverer seekers of power. This pessimistic vision of the course of history is illustrated in Parnicki's oeuvre by contrasting Christianity — a "dream" centered around the perfect half-breed: God-man — to the established Church, and by setting the legends about "Counter-Earth" against the cruelty of the conquistadores.

One can find in Parnicki's oeuvre several other detailed thematic motifs, for example, strained son-father relations, and one of them is particularly revealing for the "mutual interdependence of the creator and his characters." In nearly all the novels a scene appears in which a woman takes off her shoes and walks barefoot. The frequency of this motif gives the impression that the scene has a special — certainly erotic — significance for the author. Indeed, he tells in the autobiographical part of *The Muse* how deeply he was moved as an adolescent in Kharbin when watching a girl much older than he take off her boots after a heavy rain and wade barefoot in the puddles. The realization that such half-forgotten memories influence the reconstruction of past events (the scene in which Predslava walks barefoot to meet Bolesław in conquered Kiev, in *The New Fable*) may have strengthened Parnicki's growing conviction that practically all of history is a projection of one's own experiences into the past. In a more theoretical way, the manner in which his reconstruction proceeds has been formulated as follows (*Earthen Jugs*): "would it be so that the degree of plausibility of a [historical] guess depends on the ability of its author to become fascinated by just this guess? Incontestably."[9]

This kind of reflection on writing about history marks a turning point in the evolution of Parnicki's oeuvre. His later books, those written around 1970 and thereafter, gradually abandon the question: "why did this and this happen?" in real or imaginary history, and turn to the autothematic problem: "why was such and such event described by me in just this fashion?" The reader receives some clues: fragments of Parnicki's autobiography. A characteristic passage in *We Stood* states that "the novel *We Stood There Like Two Dreams* has as its subject . . . a search for the answer, just why . . . it bears the title *We Stood There Like Two Dreams*";[10] and toward the end of the book (p. 674) it is hinted that the pronoun "we" of the title could encompass two "I's": that of the author and that of the "ideal reader."

It is obvious that Parnicki has exchanged the pleasures of *reconstruction* for those of *construction*. By showing openly that he is the demiurge who shapes and reshapes a world, he invited the reader to join him in the game of discovering the rules by which his creation is governed. It should also become clear that the notion of "central ideas" is valid only for the first part of the oeuvre, that is, before *Kill Cleopatra*, in which the distinction between reality and its perception, however thin, is still retained. In the second part, where reality turns out to be merely a projection of the perceiving mind, no ideas may be communicated anymore: when *signifiant* and *signifié* blend into each other, the signs cease to be signs and become only a pattern — a pattern which doesn't stand for something else but simply is there for its own sake, like a game of chess.

There is no generic name for the work of Parnicki regarded *in toto* and for that reason the slightly pretentious word "oeuvre" has been used. There is likewise no suitable term for his "novels," especially the later ones, unless one were to accept the definition given by S.I. Witkiewicz (1885 - 1939): a bag into which anything may be stuffed. Parnicki himself proposed in *The Muse* and elsewhere the term "romance" in the old sense, that is, fiction describing that which never happened. This term is also unsuitable, even ridiculous, and chiefly because in Parnicki's later works nothing at all happens. They are a blend of diary and essay, presented as learned puzzles, and camouflaged as dialogues.

The reason for these terminological difficulties is that Parnicki's oeuvre is in a way unique. He has an affinity with Borges and Nabokov, but without the succinctness of the first or the brilliance of the second. His prose is often rambling, tedious and muddled by *longeurs* which are for many readers intolerable. Judging by the number of their editions, only three of his novels are popular and significantly these three are his early works: *Aetius, Silver Eagles,* and *Only Beatrice.*[11] But he also has passionate partisans who resemble members of an esoteric sect.

His oeuvre as a whole resembles chess because of its greatness and its emptiness. Both these traits are unmistakable. Although the core of his puzzles may sometimes appear naïve or outright silly, their construction is admirable and it is by this last quality that his work should be judged.[12] His cherished ambition, as he often repeats, has always been to revive historical fiction. In a way he has done this, not so much by having introduced the fantastic element, but rather by having created a new brand of obscurity. He is a master in imparting to the reader a feeling for the dazzling complexity, ambiguity, and suspect nature of history, or in fact, of being. It has been said that "after having read twenty pages of Parnicki one starts to doubt one's own existence"[13] and this is not greatly exaggerated.

Parnicki's work seems to be on the verge of total chaos, but at the same time the reader feels that there is pattern to it, even if he cannot grasp it, because the author is always a few jumps ahead. This feeling explains the difficult fascination of this strange collection of "reading material" (one of Parnicki's own terms; another one is "mirabilium"). It is the feeling of challenge. Here is a fully self-sufficient world, created and supported by a living mind — in fact *being* a mind — and the only way to penetrate it seems to be to identify oneself completely with its creator: an impossible task or a dangerous venture.

University of Louvain

NOTES

1. *Aetius, the Last Roman*, tr. J. Avisov (Moscow: Progress, 1969).
2. More exhaustive accounts of Parnicki's biography, although deliberately vague as concerns the 1939 - 41 period, are given in *Słownik współczesnych pisarzy polskich* (Warsaw: PWN, 1964), vol. 2, p. 619 f. and Z. Lichniak, "W strone Parnickiego" in T. Parnicki, *Szkice literackie* (Warsaw: Pax, 1978), pp. 5 - 73. Some information may also be found in M. Czermińska, *Teodor Parnicki* (Warsaw: PWN, 1974); A. Chojnacki, Parnicki. *W labiryncie historii* (Warsaw: PWN, 1975); T. Parnicki, *Rodowód literacki* (Warsaw: Pax, 1974); the extended version of this book appeared recently as *Historia w literaturę przekuwana* (Warsaw: Czytelnik, 1980).
3. *Teodor Parnicki* (1974), p. 7.
4. *Zabij Kleopatrę* (1968), p. 292.
5. A. Kozak, "Wybrane problemy składniowe powieści Teodora Parnickiego 'Tylko Beatrycze'," *Acta Universitatis Wratislaviensis,* 1975, no. 298, pp. 195 - 222.
6. Z. Mocarska, "Aluzje literackie w powieści Teodora Parnickiego 'I u możnych dziwny'," *Zeszyty Naukowe Uniwersytetu M. Kopernika,* 1972, no. 48, pp. 123 - 35.
7. See Parnicki's interview of 1971 ("Rozmowa z Teodorem Parnickim. Rozmawiał Wojciech Jamroziak," *Nurt,* 1971, no. 1): "When I was writing *Kill Cleopatra* I suddenly realized that all my books could be unified into one big cycle. And for that reason the following books — i.e. *A Different Life of Cleopatra,* which is a continuation of *Kill Cleopatra,* the sixth volume of *The New Fable, Identify* and *The Muse of Far Voyages* — were

written with the deliberate intention of forming one unified whole in many volumes, based — among other things — on the same set of characters" Quoted from M. Czermińska's *Teodor Parnicki* [1974], p. 163).
8. *Gliniane dzbany* (1966), p. 426.
9. Ibid., p. 424.
10. *Staliśmy jak dwa sny* (1973), p. 303.
11. Until 1980, six, nine, and five editions respectively.
12. See M. Ksiażak-Czermińska, "Sposoby kształtowania fikcji w powieściach historycznych Parnickiego na przykładzie 'Srebrnych orłów' i 'Nowej basni'. Styl i kompozycja." *Konferencje teoretyczno-literackie w Toruniu i Ustroniu* (Wroclaw, 1965), pp. 206 - 15.
13. M. Broński, "Muza Teodora Parnickiego," *Kultura* (Paris), 1972, no. 4, p. 295.

THE PARTY GUIDANCE OF A SOVIET LITERATURE: THE CASE OF THE UKRAINE, 1968 - 1975

VICTOR SWOBODA

The principle that the Communist Party of the Soviet Union guides Soviet literature is widely known. This guidance has been largely to its own satisfaction, since the majority of Soviet writers are Party members themselves, while those writers whose works are regularly and extensively printed are practically all Party members. It ought to simplify matters that those to be guided are themselves members of the body whose task it is to do the guiding. What is more, six well-known writers — Markov, Sholokhov, Chakovskii, Gribachev, Honchar, and Simonov — belong to the highest governing bodies of the Communist Party of the Soviet Union, while another forty-five occupy similar positions in the Party leadership at the level of the Union Republics. All this would seem to go a long way towards ensuring the production of correct Socialist Realist works; but if, nevertheless, an author submits for publication something deviating from the Party line or from the principles of Socialist Realism, there are further safeguards: the work can be stopped by the editor of a journal or of a publishing house, by the publisher's reader (*retsenzent*), or, finally, by the Glavlit censor. Each of these is a Party member skilled in ideological work and specifically entrusted with the task of preventing the publication of any ideologically unacceptable writing. Censors perfect their political "sense" in almost daily special internal seminars and possess in addition a voluminous confidential reference work, *Index of Information Not to be Published in the Open Press,* colloquially known in the trade as the *Talmud,* listing specific subjects, topics, facts, names, etc. which must not be mentioned.[1] And yet many works suffer Party criticism only *after* their appearance in print; either their deviation from the Party line remains unnoticed during the several prepublication checks, or the Party line itself changes after publication.

The Party guidance of literature may be either prescriptive or proscriptive. The Party encourages certain themes and types: the worker of today and the scientific and technological revolution are "in," as opposed to, say, historical themes or the rural past. Editors feel obliged to publish works on the "in" themes even if they are mediocre artistically; this ideological favoritism results in the denunciation by Party functionaries of some works for artistic greyness and feebleness. The prescriptive facet of the guidance is well-known, even predictable, whereas a study of the proscriptive occurrences, the Party criticism of published works deemed deviate from the norm, is much more illuminating as regards the principles of the guidance of literature.

An extreme example, and yet a typical one, is the book *O Ukraine, Our Soviet Land* (1970) by Petro Shelest.[2] A literary work, it shares at least one important feature with several fiction and nonfiction works which suffered a similar fate. The fact that Shelest is (or was) not a "writer" does not disqualify his case; besides, a man of letters is said to have ghosted his book.[3] Given the author's position — Brezhnev's opposite in the Ukraine — the censor was presumably unable to query anything. In 1971 Shelest's position assured glowing reviews, among them some signed by such notables as Ivan Bilodid, Iurii Smolych, Valentyn Rechmedin, and several others.[4] It was nearly a year after his removal from office that the book was vehemently attacked in an anonymous editorial article (widely attributed to his successor, Volodymyr V. Shcherbyts'kyi) in *Komunist Ukraïny.*[5] Among "serious shortcomings and errors" noted were these: the idealization of the Zaporozhian Sech as "some sort of 'absolute' democracy"; failure to mention the advantages gained by the Ukraine from being joined to Russia in the seventeenth century; tracing the Ukraine's history in isolation from that of Russia; and failure to show the beneficial effect of Russian culture upon Ukrainian culture. "Altogether," the anonymous writer sums up, "the book stresses too much the peculiarities and singularity of the history and culture of the Ukrainian people." Shelest paid dearly for deviating from the Party line, and so apparently did his ghost writer. The specific charges against Shelest, "leaked" to Western correspondents, were never published in the Soviet Union, and, apart from some vague accusations, the most serious attacks on him are contained in the *Komunist Ukraïny* editorial article.

A similar episode, the first one of its kind after Stalin, had occurred only three years before the publication of Shelest's book in the affair with Oles' Honchar's *The Cathedral*. He was First Secretary or Chairman of the Writers' Union of the Ukraine (WUU in the following) for a decade,[6] a member of the Central Committee of the Communist Party of the Ukraine and an alternate member of the Central Committee of the Communist Party of the Soviet Union. His many novels, published in large editions, had regularly won official acclaim, so that *The Cathedral* was unlikely to have come under close scrutiny before its publication, first in the prestigious Kiev monthly *Vitchyzna,* then in a paperback edition of 100,000 copies in January 1968, and two or three months later in a hardback edition.[7] Quite predictably, the novel was greeted with unadulterated praise, both in Kiev and in the provinces, chiefly in the periodicals of the industrial southeast, since the setting of the novel is transparently the Dnepropetrovsk area.[8] Within less than four months after its publication, the Party ideologists realized that the novel was "ideologically faulty": it harked back to the old Cossack tradition, idealized the Zaporozhian Sech as "the Christian Cossack republic," neglected the "class approach," and employed a cathedral built by Cossacks as a symbol linking the past and the present. This turnabout in the Party line occurred exactly at the time of Honchar's jubilee. A glowing tribute to *The Cathedral* had appeared in *Literaturna Ukraïna,*[9] the organ of the executive board of the WUU, and *The*

Cathedral was mentioned with approval in the center spread of the same paper. The next evening, on April 3, 1968, there was a festive soiree at the Kiev Conservatory in Honchar's honor at which Leonid Novychenko read a paper on Honchar's work.[10] In his speech of thanks Honchar revealed that he had learnt about moves "to pin a label," in the style of Stalin's times, on *The Cathedral,* and defiantly declared: "I regard this work as being no less patriotic than *The Standard Bearers*. . . . Just as all my previous works, *The Cathedral* was written from Leninist and internationalist positions." These words were greeted, according to the *samizdat* transcript, with "a storm of prolonged applause."[11]

But in the Dnepropetrovsk daily *Zoria* a lambasting article, complete with a worker's signature, and entitled "I See Life Differently," appeared three days after Honchar's fiftieth birthday,[12] to be followed by several others published in the same city. Because of a delay in the announcement of the new Party line on *The Cathedral* to provincial editors and censors, another favorable review was published in the city of Lutsk, in the northwest.[13] Subsequent attacks appeared in Kiev and even in Moscow.[14]

But *The Cathedral's* popularity among its readers was undiminished. A Russian translation appeared in *samizdat,* and a Polish translation — without commentary — was made available by the State Publishing Institute in early 1972. (So far, a translation into German remains the one and only complete rendering into a Western language.)[15] The press campaign against *The Cathedral* died down within ten weeks, but there were other repercussions. Several people who refused to accept the new April Party line and defended *The Cathedral* paid for this by losing their jobs and being expelled from, or penalized by, the Party or the Communist Youth League. The author of an anonymous *samizdat* document detailing these facts was traced and imprisoned for four and a half years.[16]

The book itself was withdrawn from sale and from libraries, and was no longer mentioned in print except in certain bibliographical contexts. But it was criticized at least twice in the same year at Party meetings of Kiev writers: on April 29, Dr. Novychenko admonished that it was "possible to have different attitudes to *The Cathedral* [viz., also favourable ones]" and on December 16, Honchar reasserted that he had written it "with the patriotic feelings of a Soviet writer."[17] In 1971, Honchar lost his chairmanship of the WUU.

Elements of this specifically Ukrainian pattern can be seen in several other cases when works were found ideologically unacceptable after publication and their authors berated for their idealization of Cossackdom and the Zaporozhian Sech. V.I. Zaremba's biographical novel on a late nineteenth-century poet, Ivan Manzhura, was first reviewed favorably in 1972, but attacked several times early in 1973 for "anti-historical fabrications."[18] The last extensive review, by A. Tutyk, appeared in the Kiev Russian-language literary monthly *Raduga*. Zaremba's book is classified as "ideologically immature." "Instead of describing the period [the late nineteenth century, when Manzhura lived] in some depth, the author transports the reader into the seventeenth-eighteenth centuries, into Cossack times. Moreover, he deliberately views the Ukraine's distant past one-sidedly and embellishes Cossackdom. Zaremba at times forgets about their [the Cossacks'] social heterogeneity.... The Cossacks' class struggle...recedes in Zaremba's treatment into the background.... For what purpose did Zaremba need such lack of objectivity?.... Is it to show that the Ukraine's griefs and misfortune were brought by other [viz. Russian], never its own, Ukrainian, feudal lords?"[19]

Another biographical novel, on an early nineteenth-century writer Kvitka-Osnov"ianenko, by I. Il'ienko, was attacked by S. Shakovs'kyi for idealizing the Ukrainian gentry and Cossack chiefs, and for describing the last Zaporozhian ataman Petro Kalnyshevs'kyi (imprisoned in the Solovki Islands in 1775) as "a true martyr," "a real Zaporozhian knight." An anonymous "reviewer" objected to the fact that for Il'ienko there was only one important aspect of the activity and the outlook of the various nineteenth-century historical personages populating his book, viz., their attitude toward the Ukrainian language and literature and toward the cultural and educational work of Kvitko-Osnov"ianenko and his Kharkov friends. Two months later, Il'ienko had to admit publicly that he had dwelt too much on the descriptions of the lives of some of the Ukrainian gentry and Cossack chiefs, but he passed over in silence the other two charges.[20]

When M. Kytsenko's *The Island of Khortytsia: Heroism and Legends*[21] appeared in 1967, one reviewer described him as "a brilliant expert on the history of Cossackdom,"[22] while another, writing in an academic journal, considered "that it would not be a mistake to classify Kytsenko's work among the best popularizing scholarly essays of the historical genre."[23] But his second edition, published five years later, was cited in the same journal, for "serious shortcomings," in particular for the "idealization of the social order of the Zaporozhian Sech"; also Olena Apanovych's foreword was condemned because in it "the democratic order which allegedly reigned in the Sech is excessively idealized."[24]

Similar errors were found in A. Karpenko's study of Gogol''s populism (*narodnost'*), where Gogol''s sources in folklore are traced. According to two reviewers of Karpenko's work, the folklore idealizes and exaggerates democracy and social justice among the Cossacks; and "this [folklore] theme of self-government in its idealized form was in part accepted by Gogol'" in his *Taras Bul'ba*. Karpenko's "sad error" lies in the fact that he "does not stress the problem of the idealization of the theme of Cossack self-government, nor does he stress the fact that 'communal democratism' in the Zaporozhian Sech was actually a powerless phenomenon in the face of the omnipotence and despotism of the Zaporozhian hetmans and chiefs and the Cossack ruling strata."[25]

One "historical" novel, Ivan Bilyk's *The Sword of Ares*,[26] alarmed Party critics to a remarkable degree. An utterly fantastic fiction set in the fourth and fifth centuries, it identifies the Huns with the Slavs and Attila with the Kievan Prince Bohdan Hatylo, shifting his capital from Buda to Kiev. The life of Bilyk's Slavs is modelled on Kiev in the tenth to thirteenth centuries and on the Cossacks in the sixteenth to eighteenth centuries. He derived this metamorphosis chiefly from the equally fantastic work of a mid-nineteenth-century historian, A. Vel'tman, who devoted Chapter 3 of his *Attila and Rus' of the Fourth and Fifth Centuries* to proving the equation, *Kyiane* (Kievites) = *Quenae/Chueni* = *Hunni* (Huns). The title of Chapter 4, "Attila, the Grand Prince of Kiev and Autocrat of All the Russias" (Attila, velikii kniaz' Kievskii i vseia Rusi samoderzhets)[27] speaks for itself. The sincerity of Bilyk's belief in this fantasy was matched by the shrillness of his numerous detractors. Bilyk's novel was criticized at a meeting of the WUU Commission on Criticism on October 17, 1972. This meeting was meant to be a summing up of the improvements in literary criticism expected after the publication of the directive of the Central Committee of the CPSU of January 21, 1972, "On Literary and Art Criticism."[28] But only one monthly, the *Zhovten'* of Lvov, was examined, and it was noted that *The Sword of Ares* was marked by an erroneous and antischolarly treatment of the events of the distant past, and that it needed a thorough, not just cursory, analysis.[29] At about the same time, at a meeting of the Executive Board of the Kiev Organization of the WUU, ideological and artistic mistakes in Bilyk's novel were pointed out, while the Board's chairman, Iurii Zbanats'kyi, regretted that the Prose Section of the WUU had failed to examine the work when it was still in manuscript.[30] The analysis materialized in the shape of an article, "Contrary to the Truth of History" by P. Tolochko, in which Bilyk's cavalier treatment of history is shown.[31] At a joint meeting of the Party organizations of the Kiev monthlies *Vitchyzna* and *Vsesvit* "the loss of class bearings" was added to the charges against *The Sword of Ares*,[32] while I. Dzeverin brought forward another accusation: the novel was "ideologically faulty and written not without some influence from bourgeois nationalist 'theories'."[33] All this criticism failed to exact a public recantation from Bilyk, and the newly elected First Secretary of the WUU remarked impatiently at a plenum of the WUU Executive Board: "It is high time for the writer Ivan Bilyk to think and draw serious conclusions for himself from the criticism which has been directed against the novel *The Sword of*

Ares, written from nationalist historico-methodological positions. For this matter is considerably more serious than the author and some of his novel's defenders pretend."[34] Disapproval from an even higher level was voiced in the anti-Shelest article: "In recent years, a number of books (by R. Ivanychuk, S. Plachynda, I. Bilyk) have appeared . . . whose characteristic is the idealization of patriarchalism [viz., things past]."[35] Finally, the anonymous "reviewer" spelled out the substance of the two most serious charges: a "loss of class bearings" manifest in the idyllic relations between the rulers and the ruled in Bilyk's Slav/Hun society, and the idea of the superiority and exclusiveness of the Hun/Slav/Ukrainian nation, which "is alien to the [Ukrainian] people; and if it is 'needed' by anyone today it is by its enemies — the Ukrainian bourgeois nationalists."[36]

The fate of *Hollyhocks,* a historical novel by R. Ivanychuk, mentioned above, was not so straightforward. The novel was serialized in 1968, favorably reviewed, and had two editions[37] before it was noted that, although set in the Crimean Khanate between 1640 and 1650, the novel ignored the impending 1654 union of the Ukraine with Russia, as was pointed out in 1970 in the main Russian language daily of the Party in the Ukraine.[38] However, the novel was praised without any reservations several months later.[39] Even more surprisingly, a certain ambiguity was heard in statements by a high WUU functionary, Pavlo Zahrebel'nyi, at the Sixth WUU Congress in May 1971, when he referred to "the sparklingly sharp Roman Ivanychuk (*Hollyhocks*)," and yet had "to note with regret that Roman Ivanychuk had not thought through the idea of his, on the whole talented, novel *Hollyhocks.*"[40] After the January 1972 CPSU Central Committee directive on criticism, the monthly *Zhovten'* was reproved for not having published any proper critique of *Hollyhocks;*[41] in April 1973 Ivanychuk's name appeared in the anti-Shelest article mentioned above, and later the same month or in early May he was placed on the censorship's secret list of "un-persons."[42] About October, the ban on him must have been lifted, as from December onwards his stories began appearing in periodicals,[43] as well as further attacks on *Hollyhocks*.[44] Finally, the offending novel was removed from the article on Ivanychuk in a biobibliographical reference work published in 1976, as were three other titles listed in earlier editions.[45] Ivanychuk's fortunes took another turn for the better when he was awarded a prize for the best novel of 1978.[46]

The formula "opposing the past to the present," used in the anti-Shelest article to condemn the three writers, was used once more a month later in the same journal, this time by M. Shamota, the top ideologist in Soviet Ukrainian literary scholarship in an attack on R. Fedoriv's "The Turkish Bridge" published more than two years earlier.[47] What Shamota found objectionable was Fedoriv's dictum that a patriot is one who loves and respects the past; even more objectionable for Shamota was the assertion by one character that a spirit of freedom and patriotism reigned in the Zaporozhian Sech, while another added that anyone who disagrees is not a patriot. From this, in Shamota's ominous words, "it is not far to opposing the old to the new."[48] A year later the presidium of the WUU Executive Board was still uneasy about the subjectivism and classless approach to historical processes shown by Ivanychuk in *Hollyhocks* and by Fedoriv in "The Turkish Bridge."[49]

Another target for denunciation by Shamota was Iu. Kolisnychenko's and S. Plachynda's *The Burning Bush,* published in 1968, but only Plachynda's name was mentioned in the anti-Shelest article.[50] The book consists of biographical sketches of six eighteenth-century Ukrainians, and Shamota objected to the way "a thoroughly mythical picture is created of the prosperity and flowering of the Ukraine up to a certain period. Moreover, the flowering and prosperity of the landowners are made to pass for the flowering of the country and its people." Not only that, Shamota continues, but also "throughout the book are scattered allusions insulting to our northern neighbor [Russia] regarding backwardness, savagery, stupidity, and so on. It is said more than once that there was no reunification of the two peoples [viz., the 1654 alliance, or joining, of the Eastern Ukraine to Russia], and that at that time Russia and Poland simply partitioned the Ukraine between themselves." Shamota sums up the chief idea of *The Burning Bush* as "the concept of the Ukraine's flowering prior to the reunification and decline after it."[51] Like Ivanychuk's works, *The Burning Bush* was subsequently removed from the 1976 bibliography.

The case of Borys Kharchuk shows how long a "deviating" work may escape detection, and how much a matter of chance its detection may be. In December 1967 or early 1968 Kharchuk brought a short story to the editor of the youth monthly *Pioneriia,* Iu. Iarmysh. Its title was "Povstans'kyi kin'" (The Insurgent's Horse); Iarmysh explained to Kharchuk that *povstans'kyi* was associated with the nationalist Ukrainian Insurgent Army, while the Soviet guerrillas were known as "partisans" (*partyzany*). Kharchuk mentioned that the story had already appeared under that title in a prestigious daily, but nonetheless he changed *povstantsi* to *partyzany* and the story was published in the *Pioneriia.*[52] Five years later Iarmysh came across "The *Insurgent's* Horse" in a recent collection of Kharchuk's short stories[53] (in the text "insurgents" had been changed, except in one place, to "partisans"). Iarmysh then scrutinized all the children's books written by Kharchuk in recent years and wrote a lengthy article entitled "Contrary to Life's Truth."[54] He was caused "astonishment and indignation" by, among other items, the parable-like fairy tales which Kharchuk inserted in his long short story "Little Wonder,"[55] and which appeared to Iarmysh to have "a double meaning and distorted hints at reality." A particularly shocking example depicted a "Princess of the Fields" (*kniazivna-polivna*) with a magic well and a magic cherry tree, an allegorical personification of the Ukraine, knights, her sons (Cossacks), Tsar Terrible, and King Pompous. Desirous of obtaining the Princess' magic possessions, the Tsar offers his aid during a struggle between the knights and King Pompous (Poland). But he cannot make use of her possessions without the magic word which the Princess refuses to disclose. She is cruelly tortured, but drops dead only when her tongue (the Ukrainian language) is cut off.

For Iarmysh this was "an extremely distorted interpretation of the events during the period of the Ukrainian people's struggle against the Polish lords." At the next Party meeting of Kiev writers, the secretary of the Party Committee, B. Chalyi, declared that "Bohdan Kharchuk had committed serious errors in his work, depicting from classless positions complicated processes of the establishment of Soviet life in the western regions of the Ukraine."[56] Another review, "B. Kharchuk's Anti-Historical Exercises" by H. Konovalov,[57] provided further details of Kharchuk's transgressions, which were said to include writing "with...undisguised hatred...about the reunification," and showing "enthusiasm for abstract humanism and an illusory understanding of freedom." Konovalov illustrates the latter with a lengthy quotation from the story "Two Days,"[58] in which a lawyer, who is to defend a Communist at a political trial in the prewar Western Ukraine, muses: "Every political trial, even the smallest one, is historic. And it begins from that first distant day when the first conquerors stepped onto our land.... Justice is freedom.... The loss of liberty of one individual is the loss of liberty of the whole people. To deprive even one person of the right to think, and to take his freedom from him, means robbing the whole society of both its mind and its freedom." (Konovalov's indignation may have been caused by Kharchuk's rather transparent hint at the "concrete" political trials in the Ukraine in 1966-72 rather than by anything "abstract.") The two articles were discussed at the editorial council and the Party meeting of the Veselka Publishing House which had put out Kharchuk's offending books, and the guilty were penalized.[59]

R. Andriiashyk's "Poltva" (The River) is also set in the prewar Western Ukraine, but its deviations were discovered early enough to prevent the publication of at least a part of the novel. The first two parts of "Poltva" appeared in the Kharkov monthly *Prapor* in late 1969,[60] and the third part was scheduled for publication in 1970, but did not appear, presumably having been stopped by Party agencies, perhaps by Kozachenko himself, who in November seems to have been the first one to refer in public to "Poltva" as "a work of doubtful historical value."[61] An article attacking the novel in the Party daily *Radians'ka Ukraïna* may have been commissioned by the Party, perhaps by Kozachenko. Within a month a special joint meeting of the Commission on Criticism and the Theory of Literature of the WUU and the Section for Prose of the Kiev Writers' Organization was convened to discuss "Poltva," and another review appeared.[62] In all, the novel's chief defect was to show the Galician Ukrainians as a homogeneous group, socially and politically, and virtually to ignore the history of the working class and the Communist Party of the Western Ukraine in the 1920s.

The handling of contemporary themes was also found to be faulty in the works of several writers. I. Chendei's "Ivan" was twice attacked in 1969 for portraying, in a postwar setting, a village priest in thoroughly positive colors and a Soviet activist as a completely repugnant type. In Kozachenko's words, he "distorted the true picture of kolkhoz reality."[63] Chendei could not publish between the end of 1970 and May 1974, when he finally admitted in print that in "Ivan" he had "shown our Soviet reality in a distorted way."[64] V. Drozd's novel "Catastrophe" was scored in 1968 for depicting "the conflict of an individual with the masses on the grounds of [the individual's] superiority and exceptional nature," and for implying that "human individuality must not be subjected to any normalization by society, for then it loses its character, is levelled and dissolved in the mass."[65] L. Novychenko, who appealed for a deep analysis of the novel's complexity rather than a simplistic "either black or white" judgment of it, was unheeded. A year later, Kozachenko criticized the novel's atmosphere as "filled with hopelessness and despair," and Zahrebel'nyi in his report to the Sixth WUU Congress declared that Drozd was unable to solve the problem of the relationship between his hero and the collective."[66] V. Maniak is another author whose treatment of contemporary Soviet life appeared objectionable to Kozachenko, who, over three years after the publication of the story "Eureka," found the author "poking fun at the socio-patriotic ritual in the life of a factory collective and making "assertions about the levelling of personality in our society."⁶⁷

Mykola Rudenko, whose subsequent fate as a founder and leader of the Ukrainian Helsinki Group became known in the West, was first criticized by Shamota in 1973 for a tendency (said not to be confined to Rudenko alone) "to poeticize the village as a spiritual haven for the lonely human being exhausted by the city bustle, and as a source of national self-awareness," where, as in Rudenko's collection of lyrics, *Rebirth,* the hero is sent "to regain his moral health."⁶⁸ L. Sanov levelled more serious charges against an earlier poetry collection, *The Universe in Thee,* finding in it " 'homilies' written from the positions of 'Christian' idealism," while other poems were "ideologically defective," imbued with antisocial views and an intolerance for kolkhoz reality and our contemporary life.⁶⁹ Sanov's charges were perhaps dictated by the need to blacken the character of Rudenko, who in January 1972 had sent a letter to the Party which was classified as hostile by the prosecution at his trial in June and July 1977. He was sentenced then to a total of twelve years, having already been expelled from the Party in 1974, and from the WUU in June 1975.⁷⁰ Oles' Berdnyk, also a founder of the Ukrainian Helsinki Group and its leader after Rudenko's arrest, was also expelled from the WUU, in May 1973, and sentenced in late 1979 to a total of nine years.⁷¹ In 1972, his science fiction novel *Astral Corsair* was belatedly criticized by, among others, M. Lohvynenko, who found in it a longing for the Cossack past.⁷² In 1970, a number of his science fiction works had been found to contain mysticism and idealism, that is, religiousness thinly disguised.⁷³

Religiousness should be, as a rule, easily discovered before publication, and indeed, examples of this transgression are few; they include D. Herasymchuk's short story "I, Who Am Going. . . ." (1971) which was declared after two and a half years' delay to contain idealized childhood reminiscences with a strong religious flavor;⁷⁴ and M. Medunytsia's short story "Colored Crayons," condemned by Sanov after a similar delay for portraying an artist who had in childhood a passion for painting icons of the

Virgin Mary.[75]

Literary works, after being criticized, either by Party agencies within or outside the WUU or by individual critics following the Party line, and depending on the seriousness of the charges, may be withdrawn and deleted from bibliographical reference works; sometimes the writers are not published anymore, but they may be readmitted into print, sometimes after a suitable public recantation (Chendei); and, as a rule, no more ideologically dubious works by them appear after that.

The period outlined above began with an event unprecedented in the post-Stalin era, a critical attack on the holder of the highest office in a Republic's Writers' Union; Honchar's experience was not to prove unique: Ivan Chendei, who was for many years the First Secretary of the Transcarpathian Branch of the WUU, similarly displeased the Party, and he, too, subsequently lost his WUU office. His successor, Iurii Meihesh, was found guilty of the advocacy of anticollectivism in his *Today and Always (A Literary Mosaic),* as well as of using the proscribed "modernist" (Western) "stream of consciousness" technique.[76] Other writers occupying ideologically important posts also diverged from the Party line in their works, for example, Roman Fedoriv, for many years the editor-in-chief of *Zhovten'.*

There was a noticeable hardening of the Party line subsequent to the January 1972 directive of the Central Committee of the CPSU on literary and art criticism; a major onslaught was started in the same month against Ukrainian dissidents and *samizdat;* several writers and critics were among those who fell victim to that wave of arrests, including the critics Ivan Svitlychnyi and Ievhen Sverstiuk. The hardening of the line was carried even further in the wake of the anti-Shelest campaign and culminated in the editorial article in *Komunist Ukraïny* of April 1973.

The most important deviation scored by the Party was enthusiasm or nostalgia for the Cossack era, with its associations to past glory, freedom, national independence, and resentment for their loss. The treatment of other periods of history, as well as of contemporary conditions in the Ukraine, may also fail to satisfy the Party critics, sometimes because of "distorted national feelings." Some other charges made by Party critics, especially against writings set in the present (the "misrepresentation of Soviet reality," offences against the principles of Socialist Realism or against obligatory optimism), are not specific to the Ukraine. This could also be said when religious tendencies are unmasked.

Towards the end of the period surveyed there was a greater vigilance at the prepublication stage, so that fewer works had to be criticized for heresy, but more for being monotonous, grey, and uninteresting. Zahrebel'nyi's remarks at the December 1975 plenum of the WUU Executive Board are noteworthy in this connection:

> One is struck by an astonishing monotony in the overwhelming majority of our journalistic works. Some incomprehensible levelling of creative individualities is taking place. Even capable writers, with established reputations, when they set about writing essays, seem to lose their creative nerve and abdicate all artistic ambition. This moreover refers not only to prose but, what is quite incredible, also even to poetry![77]

The genre of "journalistic essay," as opposed to fiction, is greatly encouraged, and fiction writers have continuously been urged to take it up; the mention of poetry is obviously a reference to "civic" poetry, which has also been promoted at the expense of lyric poetry.

The hardening of the Party line in the final years of the period is also demonstrated in the treatment of writers no longer alive. Thus, Vasyl' Symonenko (1935-1963) was greatly esteemed for his "high Communist principles" (*vysoka komunistychna ideinist'*) and as "an example of service to his people," a monument to him was unveiled on the fourth anniversary of his death, a number of unpublished poems were printed in 1968-69, a collection of his satirical and humorous verse was planned for publication in 1969 or shortly afterwards, and a deluxe edition of his verse and prose was to be published in 1972.[78] Neither of these two latter publications appeared, and in February 1974 Shamota declared him guilty of "an exaggerated or distorted display of national feelings."[79] Soon after this, the hitherto unassailable classic, Ivan Franko (1856-1916), was toppled from his pedestal. He had been seen as "a consistent revolutionary democrat and Marxist," but now it was emphasized that from 1883 on he abandoned the workers' movement and turned all his attention to the village.[80]

Even Taras Shevchenko (1814-1861), the undisputed revolutionary democrat, habitually described as a poet of genius and the founder of modern Ukrainian literature, has not escaped unscathed. In 1974 several poems were excised from *Kobzar,* which is traditionally Shevchenko's *complete* poetry.[81] The poems condemn Russia's annexation of the Ukraine; essentially the same poems were also cut in the early 1950s, under Stalin, but restored after his death,[82] and most of them had likewise displeased the Tsarist censorship and the Third Department of His Imperial Majesty's Chancellery. History has come full circle once again.

University of London

NOTES

1. Leonid Vladimirov, "*Glavlit:* How the Soviet Censor Works," *Index on Censorship,* vol. 1, no. 3/4 (1972), pp. 38-39.
2. Petro Iu. Shelest, *Ukraïno nasha Radians'ka* (Kiev: Vydavnytstvo Politychnoï literatury Ukraïny, 1970).
3. His name seems not to have been mentioned in print, and it may be inopportune to do so.
4. Ivan K. Bilodid, "Velych revoliutsiinykh zvershen'," *Druh chytacha,* March 16, 1971; Iurii K. Smolych, "Spriamovanist' u maibutnie," *Literaturna Ukraïna* (*LU* in the following), March 12, 1971; Valentyn O. Rechmedin, "Shliakh rozkvitu, shchastia i slavy," *Radians'ke literaturoznavstvo,* 1971, no. 8, pp. 3-6; Oleksa Ie. Nosenko ("Velichie, dobytoe trudom," *Raduga,* 1971, no. 6, pp. 170-173) is worth quoting: "The Ukrainian people were one of the first to follow deliberately the lead of their elder brother — the Russian people — in an attack on capitalism." Moreover, Vasyl' Kozachenko (see note 9 below) devoted a brief but

Party Guidance of a Literature

laudatory section to Shelest's book in his article "Nash kermanych," *LU*, March 30, 1971.

5. "Pro seriozni nedoliky ta pomylky odniei knyhy," *Komunist Ukraïny*, 1973, no. 4, pp. 77-82.

6. The highest office in the WUU carried the title First Secretary of the Executive Board of the WUU between 1966 and 1969 and since 1973, and Chairman of the Executive Board of the WUU at other times.

7. Oles' T. Honchar, "Sobor. Roman," *Vitchyzna*, 1968, no. 1, pp. 16-169; *Sobor* (Kiev: Dnipro, 1968); *Sobor* (Kiev: Radians'kyi pys'mennyk, 1968).

8. The following reviews appeared in Kiev periodicals: Marharyta Malynovs'ka, "Zhyttia v romani," *LU*, January 19, 1968; Volodymyr P"ianov, "Svitlotini chasu," *Robitnycha hazeta*, February 22, 1968; Oleksandr Diachenko, "Z liubov"iu do liudei," *Druh chytacha*, February 27, 1968; Viktor Ivanysenko, "Tvortsi i brakon'iery," *Vitchyzna*, 1968, no. 4, pp. 139-148. Those which appeared in provincial papers are the following: V. Vlasenko and Serhii Burlakov, "V nebi romanu — Dnipropetrovshchyna," *Prapor iunosti* (Dnepropetrovsk), February 13, 1968; O. Hanich, "Za sontse i holuby," *Komsomolets' Zaporizhzhia*, March 8, 1968; in Russian-language papers: I. Belogub, "Sled na zemle," *Luganskaia pravda*, February 14, 1968; Petro Symonenko, "Iz pravdy i krasoty," *Industrial'noe Zaporozh'e*, February 18, 1968. A fuller record appears in "Lyst tvorchoï molodi Dnipropetrovs'koho," *Suchasnist'*, vol. 9, no. 2 (1969), pp. 78-79.

9. Oles' Lupii, "Sobory dush liuds'kykh," *LU*, March 29, 1968.

10. Mykola Shudria and Oleksii Dmytrenko, "Chervonoho zhyta kolos," *LU*, April 5, 1968.

11. Oles' Honchar, "Slovo na vechori 3 kvitnia 1968 roku," *Journal of Ukrainian Graduate Studies*, vol. 1, no. 1 (1976), pp. 48-50.

12. H. Dihtiarenko, "Ia bachu zhyttia ne takym," *Zoria*, April 6, 1968.

13. I. Sirak, "Z shyrot zhyttia," *Radians'ka Volyn'*, April 13, 1968.

14. M. Iurchuk and F. Lebedenko, "Pered lytsem diisnosti," *Radians'ka Ukraïna*, April 26, 1968; Mykola Z. Shamota, "Realizm i pochuttia istorii," *Radians'ka Ukraïna*, May 16, 1968; N. Fed', "Dostoinstvo iskusstva," *Izvestiia*, June 13, 1968.

15. See Reddaway, *Uncensored Russia*, p. 292; Oleś Honczar, *Sobór*, tr. Kazimierz Truchanowski (Warsaw: Państwowy Instytut Wydawniczy, 1972); Olesj Hontschar, *Der Dom von Satschipljanka. Roman*, tr. Elisabeth Kottmeier and Eaghor G. Kostetzky (Hamburg: Hoffmann und

Campe, 1970).
16. "Lyst tvorchoï...," pp. 78-85; Reddaway, *Uncensored Russia*, pp. 292-294, 467-468.
17. See "Ideina zhurtovanist', boiova nastupal'nist'. Zbory pys'mennykiv-komunistiv m. Kyieva," *LU*, May 7, 1968, and "Zbory pys'mennykiv-komunistiv Kyieva," *LU*, December 20, 1968; "Na peredovi rubezhi suchasnosti! Iz zvitno-vybornykh zboriv pys'mennykiv-komunistiv Kyieva," *LU*, December 27, 1968.
18. Volodymyr I. Zaremba, *Ivan Manzhura* (Kiev: Molod', 1972). Two reviews of 1972 are the following: Ievheniia Sokhats'ka, "Zbyrach narodnykh perlyn," *LU*, May 12, 1972, and Valentyn Chemerys in *Prapor iunosti*, August 15, 1972. The first attacks of 1973 were: P. Velychko, "Koly brakuie vidchuttia istoryzmu," *Zoria*, March 25, 1973; and V. Borodin and M. Iatsenko, "Istorychna pravda i antyistorychni domysly," *Radians'ke literaturoznavstvo*, 1973, no. 4, pp. 75-79.
19. Anatolii Tutyk, "S pozitsii antiistorizma," *Raduga*, 1973, no. 6, pp. 176-181.
20. Ivan Il'ienko, *Hryhorii Kvitka-Osnov"ianenko* (Kiev: Molod', 1973). Shakhovs'kyi, "Fakty i domysly." For Il'ienko's response to the anonymous "reviewer" (Ohliadach, "Ideinist'....") see Ivan Il'ienko, "Lyst do redaktsii," *LU*, August 3, 1973.
21. M.P. Kytsenko. *Khortytsia v heroiitsi i lehendakh* (Dnepropetrovsk: Promin', 1967). For early favorable reviews see G. Zabiiaka, "Geroika Khortitsy," *Industrial'noe Zaporozh'e*, November 24, 1967; and O. Avramenko, "Nema perevodu kozats'komu rodu," *Komsomolets' Zaporizhzhia*, November 29, 1967.
22. Roman Lubkivs'kyi, "Dar liubovi, pratsi, natkhnennia," *Zhovten'*, 1970, no. 10, p. 154.
23. Olena S. Kompan's review in *Ukraïns'kyi istorychnyi zhurnal*, 1968, no. 3, p. 155.
24. M.F. Kotliar's review in *Ukraïns'kyi istorychnyi zhurnal*, 1973, no. 1, pp. 139-140.
25. A.I. Karpenko, *O narodnosti Gogolia (Khudozhestvennyi istorizm pisatelia i ego narodnye istoki)* (Kiev: Izdatel'stvo Kievskogo universiteta, 1973). A. Kulinych and I. Zaslavs'kyi, "Zmistovna robota, prykri prorakhunky," *LU*, July 20, 1973. Similar conclusions are arrived at by another reviewer, D. Chalyi, in *Radians'ke literaturoznavstvo*, 1973, no. 9, pp. 92-94.
26. Ivan Bilyk, *Mech Areia* (Kiev: Radians'kyi pys'mennyk, 1972).

27. A.T. Vel'tman, *Attila i Rus' IV i V veka. Svod istoricheskikh i narodnykh predanii* (Moscow: Universitetskaia Tipografiia, 1858).
28. "O literaturno-khudozhestvennoi kritike," in *Ob ideologicheskoi rabote KPSS. Sbornik dokumentov* (Moscow: Izdatel'stvo politicheskoi literatury, 1977), pp. 492-496.
29. "Oriientyry—partiina pryntsypovist' i boiovytist'. Komisiia krytyky SPU obhovoriuie literaturno-krytychni materialy 'Zhovtnia'," *LU,* October 20, 1972.
30. "Na pravlinni Kyïvs'koï orhanizatsii SPU," *LU,* October 20, 1972.
31. P. Tolochko, "Vsuperech pravdi istorii," *LU,* November 17, 1972.
32. "Proty antyistoryzmu v literaturi," *LU,* December 12, 1972.
33. Ihor O. Dzeverin, "Holovne—naukovist' i pryntsypovist'," *Radians'ka Ukraïna,* February 18, 1973.
34. Vasyl' Kozachenko, "Dopovid'," *LU,* March 27, 1973.
35. "Pro seriozni nedoliky...," p. 78.
36. See footnote 20 above.
37. Roman Ivanychuk, "Mal'vy. Istorychnyi roman," *Vitchyzna,* 1968, no. 4, pp. 78-126, no. 5, pp. 17-100. For a favorable review see Ihor Motorniuk, "Shchob ne v"ianuly mal'vy," *Prapor,* no. 11, pp. 94-96. Separate editions: Ivanychuk, *Mal'vy. Istorychnyi roman* (Kiev: Dnipro, 1968; and Kiev: Radians'kyi pys'mennyk, 1969.
38. N. Ravliuk, "Istoricheskii roman bez istorii," *Pravda Ukrainy,* February 2, 1970.
39. Aleksandr Kritsevyi, "Pafos chelovecheskoi svobody," *Raduga,* 1970, no. 10, pp. 177-179; Olena Apanovych, "Khudozhnist' ta istoryzm," *Zhovten',* 1970, no. 11, pp. 142-147.
40. Pavlo Zahrebel'nyi, "Novi obrii ukraïns'koï prozy," *LU,* May 20, 1971.
41. "Oriientyry..."
42. Whether the banning of Ivanychuk's name was or was not a direct consequence of his being mentioned unfavorably in the anti-Shelest article is difficult to ascertain. But the fact that his name was, at the time stated, placed on the list of "unpersons" is quite reliably attested (for understandable reasons, it would be inadvisable to publish the source).
43. The first among them were three short stories in *Zhovten',* 1973, no. 12, pp. 69-83.
44. "Problemy suchasnoho romanu," *LU,* March 22, 1974; "Hostryty slovo—zbroiu. Notatky z zasidannia prezydii pravlinnia SPU," *LU,* March 26, 1974.

45. *Pys'mennyky Radians'koï Ukraïny. Dovidnyk,* ed. Oleh V. Kylymnyk and Oleksandr I. Petrovs'kyi (Kiev: Radians'kyi pys'mennyk, 1976), p. 125; 1970, p. 163.
46. Ivanychuk, "Navesty mosty mizh pokolinniamy epokh . . ." (an interview conducted by Mykhailo Slaboshpyts'kyi), *LU,* February 15, 1980.
47. Roman Fedoriv, "Turets'kyi mist," *Dnipro,* 1970, no. 12, pp. 48-84.
48. Mykola Z. Shamota, "Za konkretno-istorychne vidobrazhennia zhyttia v literaturi," *Komunist Ukraïny,* 1973, no. 5, pp. 90-91.
49. "Hostryty slovo—zbroiu."
50. Iu. Kolisnychenko and Serhii P. Plachynda, *Neopalyma kupyna* (Kiev: Molod', 1968). See "Pro seriozni nedoliky. . . ," p. 78.
51. Shamota, "Za konkretno-istorychne vidobrazhennia. . . ," pp. 91-92. See *Pys'mennyky. . . ,* 1970, p. 345; 1976, p. 277.
52. Borys Kharchuk, "Povstans'kyi kin'," *Radians'ka Ukraïna,* December 7, 1967; *Pioneriia,* 1968, no. 4, p. 10-12.
53. Kharchuk, *Pomsta* (Kiev: Veselka, 1970).
54. Iurii Iarmysh, "Vsuperech zhyttievii pravdi. Z pryvodu ostannikh tvoriv dlia ditei Borysa Kharchuka," *LU,* September 18, 1973.
55. Kharchuk, "Horokhove chudo. Povist'," *Vitchyzna,* 1968, no. 4, pp. 27-74, and separately, Kharchuk, *Horokhove chudo* (Kiev: Veselka, 1968).
56. V. Koval', "Talant i trud—partii, narodu. Zvitno-vyborni partiini zbory pys'mennykiv Kyieva," *LU,* December 7, 1973.
57. Hennadii Konovalov, "Antyistorychni vpravy B. Kharchuka," *LU,* December 18, 1973.
58. Kharchuk, "Dva dni," in his *Materyns'ka liubov* (Kiev: Veselka, 1972).
59. M. Shevchenko, "Slidamy nashykh vystupiv," *LU,* December 28, 1973.
60. Roman Andriiashyk, "Poltva. Roman," *Prapor,* 1969, no. 8, pp. 12-50; no. 9, pp. 16-56.
61. Vasyl' Kozachenko, "Budivnyk komunizmu—heroi suchasnoï literatury," *LU,* November 20, 1970.
62. Bohdan Dudykevych, "Chysti dzherela temy v pototsi sub"iektyvizmu," *Radians'ka Ukraïna,* December 8, 1970. On the joint meeting see "Vsuperech istorychnii pravdi. Pro roman R. Andriiashyka 'Poltva'," *LU,* January 12, 1971. Subsequent criticism: I. Doroshenko, "A z pozytsii realizmu? Shche pro roman Ro. Adriiashyka 'Poltva'," *LU,* Jan-

uary 26, 1971.
63. Ivan Chendei, "Ivan," in his *Bereznevyi snih* (Kiev: Molod', 1968), pp. 3-74. Two reviews: "Diisnist' i pozytsiia pys'mennyka," *Zakarpats'ka pravda,* July 18, 1969; M. Klympotiuk, "Poza pravdoiu istoriï," *Molod' Ukraïny,* September 7, 1969. Kozachenko, "Budivnyk komunizmu..."
64. Chendei, "Vesna molodosti nashoï," *Zakarpats'ka pravda,* May 30, 1974; reprinted in *LU,* June 11, 1974.
65. Volodymyr Drozd, "Katastrofa. Roman," *Vitchyzna,* 1968, no. 2, pp. 20-107. The review: Viktor Kostiuchenko, "Koly heroi vyhadanyi," *Robitnycha hazeta,* September 6, 1968.
66. Leonid Novychenko, "Krytyka: Problemy i turboty," *LU,* October 18, 1968; Kozachenko, "Budivnyk komunizmu..."; Zahrebel'nyi, "Novi obrii..."
67. Volodymyr Maniak, "Evryka," *Dnipro,* 1967, no. 2, pp. 94-125; also in Maniak, *Zelenyi merydian. Evryka. Misiats' spokiinoho sontsia. Povisti* (Kiev: Molod', 1967); Kozachenko, "Budivnyk komunizmu..."
68. Mykola Rudenko, *Onovlennia* (Kiev: Radians'kyi pys'mennyk, 1971); Shamota, "Za konkretno-istorychne vidobrazhennia...," p. 87.
69. Rudenko, *Vsesvit u tobi* (Kiev: Radians'kyi pys'mennyk, 1968); Lazar S. Sanov, "Literaturna krytyka v pokhodi," *Radians'ke literaturoznavstvo,* 1974, no. 1, pp. 23-24.
70. *The Human Rights Movement in the Ukraine. Documents of the Ukrainian Helsinki Group 1976-1980,* ed. Lesya Verba and Bohdan Yasen (Baltimore, Washington, Toronto: Smoloskyp Publishers, 1980), pp. 203, 206, 253-254.
71. On his expulsion: "U prezydii SPU," *LU,* May 15, 1973; on his sentence: *The Human Rights Movement in the Ukraine,* p. 251.
72. Oles' Berdnyk, *Zorianyi korsar. Fantastychnyi roman* (Kiev: Radians'kyi pys'mennyk, 1971); Mykhailo Lohvynenko, "Na fantastychnykh manivtsiakh," *LU,* August 11, 1972.
73. Mykhailo Kovalenko, "Fantastyka chy mistyka?" *LU,* May 19, 1970.
74. Dmytro Herasymchuk, "Ia, shcho idu...Novela," *Dnipro,* 1971, no. 6, pp. 32-37; D. Vasylenko, "Shyrota—tse dobre. A hlybyna?" *LU,* January 15, 1974.
75 Mykhailo Medunytsia, "Kol'orovi olivtsi," *Moloda hvardiia,* September 5, 1971; Sanov, "Literaturna krytyka...," pp. 25-26.
76. Iurii Meihesh, *S'ohodni i zavzhdy. Literaturna mozaïka* (Uzhgorod: Karpaty, 1969); his critic: Shamota, "Za konkretno-istorychne vidobra-

zhennia...," pp. 88-90.

77. Pavlo Zahrebel'nyi, "Pys'mennyk i p"iatyrichka. Z dopovidi sekretaria pravlinnia SPU Pavla Zahrebel'noho na plenumi pravlinnia Spilky pys'mennykiv Ukraïny," *LU,* December 12, 1975.

78. *Novi knyhy Ukraïny. Kataloh vydan' ukraïns'koiu movoiu No. la 1972 roku* (Moscow: Mezhdunarodnaia kniga, 1971), pp. 214-215. On the movement see (RATAU), "Poetovi-patriotu," *LU,* December 19, 1967; a photograph of the monument, and another one of the participants of the unveiling meeting, *LU,* December 22, 1967. The unpublished poems: Vasyl' Symonenko, "Na bilykh koniakh proneslysia roky" [eight poems], *Vitchyzna,* 1968, no. 7, pp. 5-8; Symonenko, "Parodii, zharty, baiky" [twelve poems], *Dnipro,* 1969, no. 3, pp. 123-125, and in *Molod' Cherkashchyny,* March 13, 1969. On the humorous verse: Vasyl' Lysenko, "Zhyvi slova...," *Dnipro,* 1969, no. 3, p. 123. On the deluxe edition: *Novi knyhy Ukraïny,* pp. 214-215.

79. Mykola Shamota, "Aktual'ni pytannia literaturnoï krytyky," *LU,* February 8, 1974; an extended version, Shamota, "Aktual'ni pytannia suchasnoho radians'koho literaturoznavstva," *Radians'ke literaturoznavstvo,* 1974, no. 3, pp. 49-50.

80. Petro I. Kolesnyk, "Literaturoznavchi aberatsii," *Radians'ke literaturoznavstvo,* 1974, no. 5, pp. 57-59.

81. The cuts, which are not mentioned in any preface, footnotes, or endnotes, occur in all recent editions of *Kobzar,* or of Shevchenko's collected works (those including prose and drama as well). One of the first among them was a deluxe edition, Taras Shevchenko, *Kobzar* (Kiev: Dnipro, 1976), 575 pp., whose colophon shows December 23, 1974 as the date when its text was turned over to the printers.

82. "Velykyi l'okh" is the most significant poem.

**SCHEDULED PUBLICATIONS FROM THE
SECOND WORLD CONGRESS FOR
SOVIET AND EAST EUROPEAN STUDIES
GARMISCH - PARTENKIRCHEN, 1980**

ENGLISH-LANGUAGE PUBLICATIONS: Published for the International Committee for Soviet and East European Studies by a number of different publishers; General Editor, Roger E. Kanet, University of Illinois at Urbana-Champaign.

I. Humanities and History: Berkeley Slavic Specialties, P.O. Box 4605, Berkeley, California 94704 U.S.A.

1. East European Literature: Selected Papers from the Second World Congress for Soviet and East European Studies, edited by Evelyn Bristol, University of Illinois at Urbana-Champaign. ISBN 0-933884-26-5 (paper)

2. Russian and Eastern European History: Selected Papers from the Second World Congress for Soviet and East European Studies, edited by R.C. Elwood, Carleton University. ISBN 0-933884-28-1 (paper)

3. Religion and Communist Society: Selected Papers from the Second World Congress for Soviet and East European Studies, edited by Dennis J. Dunn, Southwest Texas State University. ISBN 0-933884-29-X (paper)

4. Russian Literature and Criticism: Selected Papers from the Second World Congress for Soviet and East European Studies, edited by Evelyn Bristol, University of Illinois at Urbana-Champaign. ISBN 0-933884-27-3 (paper)

5. Soviet Investment for Planned Industrialization, 1929-1937: Policy and Practice. Selected Papers from the Second World Congress for Soviet and East European Studies, edited by R.W. Davies, The University of Birmingham. ISBN 0-933884-32-X (paper)

II. International Relations: Pergamon Press, Inc., Maxwell House, Fairview Park, Elmsford, N.Y. 10523 U.S.A.

6. Soviet Foreign Policy and East-West Relations, edited by Roger E. Kanet, University of Illinois at Urbana-Champaign (summer, 1982, ca. 200 pp.).

III. Politics: Praeger Publishers, 521 Fifth Avenue, New York, N.Y. 10175 U.S.A.

7. Politics and Participation under Communist Rule, edited by Peter J. Potichnyj, McMaster University, and Jane Shapiro Zacek, New York State Governor's Office of Employee Relations (1982).

IV. Politics: George Allen & Unwin, P.O. Box 18, Park Lane, Hemel Hempstead, Herts HP2 4TE England.

8. Leadership Selection and Patron-Client Relations in the USSR and Yugoslavia, edited by T.H. Rigby, Australian National University, and Bohdan Harasymiw, The University of Calgary (1982).

V. Information Science: Published by Russica Publishers, Inc., 799 Broadway, New York, N.Y. 10003 U.S.A.

9. Access to Resources in the '80s: Proceedings of the First International Conference of Slavic Librarians and Information Specialists, edited by Marianna Tax Choldin, University of Illinois at Urbana-Champaign (1982, 110 pp., $7.50) ISBN 0-89830-049-5.

VI. Economics:

10. Planning, Efficiency and Development in the Soviet-Type Economies: Selected Topics, edited by Zbigniew M. Fallenbuchl, University of Windsor, and Gertrude Schroeder Greenslade, University of Virginia.

VII. Law: Martinus Nijhoff Publishers, P.O. Box 566, 2501 CN The Hague, The Netherlands.

11. Perspectives on Soviet Law for the 1980s, no. 24 in the series *Law in Eastern Europe,* edited by F.J.M. Feldbrugge and William B. Simons, Rijksuniversiteit te Leiden (1982).

VIII. Education: Published as a special issue of *Slavic and European Education Review International,* c/o Editor, Office of East/West Education, Bowling Green State University, Bowling Green, Ohio 43403 U.S.A.

12. Soviet Education Policy: Perspectives and Problems, edited by Patrick L. Alston, Bowling Green State University.

IX. Philosophy: D. Reidel Publishing Co., P.O. Box 17, Dordrecht, The Netherlands.

13. East European and Western Developments in the Philosophies of Science, Technology, Society and Human Values: Selected Papers from the Second World Congress for Soviet and East European Studies, edited by Peter P. Kirschenmann, Vrije Universiteit Amsterdam, and Andreis Sarlemijn, Technische Hogeschool Eindhoven.

GERMAN-LANGUAGE PUBLICATIONS: Published for the Deutsche Gesellschaft für Osteuropakunde in the series *Osteuropaforschung;* General Editor, Wolfgang Kasack, Universität zu Köln. All volumes published by Berlin Verlag, Pacelliallee 5, 1000 Berlin 33, Germany.

1. Politische Kultur, Nationalitäten und Dissidenten in der Sowjetunion, edited by Georg Brunner and Horst Herlemann, Universität Würzburg (summer 1982, 164 pp., DM 20,-) ISBN 3-87061-248-7.

2. Sicherheitspolitik und Internationale Beziehungen der Sowjetunion, edited by Georg Brunner and Horst Herlemann, Universität Würzburg (summer 1982, 88 pp., DM 15,-) ISBN 3-87061-249-5.

3. Modernisierungsprobleme in der Sowjetunion, edited by Georg Brunner, Universität Würzburg (1982, ca. 100 pp., DM 15,-) ISBN 3-87061-250-9.

4. Literatur und Sprachentwicklung in Osteuropa im 20. Jahrhundert, edited by Eberhard Reissner, Universität Mainz (summer 1982, 216 pp., DM 28,-) ISBN 3-87061-245-2.

5. Bildung und Erziehung in Osteuropa im 20. Jahrhundert, edited by Oskar Anweiler, Ruhr-Universität Bochum (summer 1982, 215 pp., DM 28,-) ISBN 3-87061-251-7.

6. Grundrechte und Rechtssicherheit im sowjetischen Machtbereich, edited by Georg Brunner, Universität Würzburg (summer 1982, 137 pp., DM 18,80) ISBN 3-87061-252-5.

7. Wirtschaftsrecht, Internationaler Handel und Friedliche Koexistenz aus osteuropäischer Sicht, edited by Georg Brunner, Universität Würzburg (summer 1982, 128 pp., DM 18,80) ISBN 3-87061-243-6.

8. *Wirtschaftsprobleme Osteuropas in der Analyse,* edited by Heinrich Vogel, Bundesinstitut für ostwissenschaftliche und internationale Studien (1982, ca. 280 pp., DM 38,-) ISBN 3-87061-254-1.

9. *Internationale Osteuropa-Forschung,* edited by Arnold Buchholz, Ständiges Sekretariat für Koordinierung der Bundesgeförderten Osteuropaforschung (summer 1982, 104 pp., DM 18,80) ISBN 3-87061-229-0. (This volume will also be published in English.)

10. *Kunst, Architektur und Musik in Osteuropa im 20. Jahrhundert,* edited by Hans-Jürgen Drengenberg, Freie Universität Berlin, with the cooperation of Milka Bliznakov, Virginia Polytechnic Institute and State University, John E. Bowlt, University of Texas at Austin, Joachim Braun, Bar-Ilan University, and Peter Spielmann, Museum der Stadt Bochum (1983).

FRENCH-LANGUAGE PUBLICATION: Special issue of the journal *Revue d'Études comparatives Est-Ouest: Économie, Planification, Organisation;* 27, rue Paul-Bert, 94204 Ivry/s/Seine, France.

"Europe de l'Est: Économie officielle et économies parallèles," *Revue d'Études comparatives Est-Ouest,* XII, no. 2 (June 1981).